Climbing Out of Bed

by Luke Mehall

Cover photo by Braden Gunem

Cover design by Lisa Slagle

THIS BOOK IS DEDICATED TO TOM MALLY, GEORGE SIBLEY AND ADAM LAWTON

Tom has always pushed me to write about my experiences while I am still young enough to recall them vividly. While working alongside him at Donita's Cantina in Crested Butte, Colorado he also taught me the value of treating your coworkers and fellow human beings with a high level of respect.

George has been many things to me, among those: a teacher, editor and friend. Whether he intended to or not, he set me on my life's course by encouraging me to stick with the writing path. I promise to do my best to inspire and encourage the next generation, as you have done for me.

Adam believed in my writing, and was always incredibly supportive. He encouraged me to manifest my stories and dreams, and I would not be who I am today without him. Although he is no longer with us in the flesh, his spirit continues to guide and inspire. I love you and miss you Adam.

"Come experience life as we know it, as some of you should know it."

Coming of Age by Jay-Z

CONTENTS

1. Introduction
2. Climbing After Kerouac
3. Untitled Poem, Inspired by Hartman Rocks
4. Wide Eyes, High Times and Hard Times, a Story of Climbing with Mark Grundon
5. The Way of the Couch Surfer
6. Weird and Wheeled Encounters in Hitchhiker's Space
7. This is Buildering
8. A Climber in the Winter of his Discontent
9. Somewhere in Between Dreams and Smog is Love
10. The Underwear Model Story
11. Wild Mountain Honey
12. Hammer's Time
13. Wild Tom Mally
14. Real Mountain People
15. Naked Disco Dance Party in J-Tree
16. Home is Where the Climbing is
17. Climbing Out of Bed
18. A Year in the Heart of a Climber
19. Mary Jane, a Climber's Thoughts on the Legalization of Marijuana
20. Trying to Hang with Ben Johnson
21. The Black Canyon, a Poem
22. Zen Dishwashing
23. The Freedom Mobile
24. Last Thoughts on Adam Lawton
25. Indian Creek Reflection, Before it All Slips Away

1 INTRODUCTION

I moved to the mountains of Colorado in 1999, a depressed twenty year old, with a deep and desperate yearning for something new. I'd already attended two colleges in my home state of Illinois, and neither one suited me. I was a lost soul that floated out to the mountains, with a very vague notion of why I did so.

That year I enrolled at my third place of higher education, Western State College of Colorado in Gunnison. At first, I didn't even actually understand what a liberal arts college was, or if I belonged there, but I was accepted and began taking classes. Equally important, I took a job as a dishwasher at a local restaurant, where I began making friends.

At Western State, and in the Gunnison Valley, I came into my own, in my own way, my mistakes and real life experiences teaching me as much, or more, than I learned in the classroom. I had teachers that inspired and encouraged me to write prose and poetry, and others that taught me how to mountain bike, kayak, ice climb, and make snow caves. If I felt like it, I took a semester off and lived in a tent; my major was Recreation, so I counted it as field experience.

The most important development within my young soul was that I got into rock climbing, and met a community that shared this passion. Climbing seemed to give me everything I needed during those years: a sense of purpose, confidence, strength, real, raw experience and a connection and deep appreciation for nature.

The first words I ever wrote that I was proud of were after a climbing trip, poetry that seemed to channel directly from my soul. The best friends I have in life are those that I've climbed with, and trusted my life to on the other end of a rope. The most vivid, sacred memories I have are from my climbing experiences. I am who I am because of climbing.

Climbing encourages travel, and travel we would, to Wyoming, Utah, California, Oregon, Mexico; anywhere with good climbing was worth the journey. Traveling is addicting, yet the more I stayed out on the road, the more I realized how important home was. The Gunnison Valley, which includes both Gunnison and Crested Butte, was home for many years, and now my home is Durango, just a few hours southwest. The Gunnison Valley is never far from my thoughts though, and rarely do I go more than a few months without visiting there.

My journey as a writer has proved as important as my climbing path, and they are intertwined. Here, in *Climbing Out of Bed*, are some of my best stories from the last thirteen years. Though nearly every story involves climbing in one way or another, there are also stories of mountain town culture, couch surfing, hitchhiking, buildering, road tripping and friendship. I've included a couple poems as well, as writing poetry can be the purest way to express emotion.

In addition to writing about climbing, I've always been drawn to write about love: the loss of love, the yearning for love and being in love. I love climbing, and I love women. What else can I say?

The third main theme of this book, in addition to climbing and love, is humor. It's impossible to climb or love without humor. I choose my climbing partners for various reasons: safety, skills, strength, etc., but I could never climb consistently with someone who didn't share a sense of humor.

That's a part of why I titled this book the way I did, and the title, I think, delivers all the themes from the writing that is presented here: climbing, humor and love. It's also a saying I've always liked, one I learned from some of the older climbers in the Gunnison Valley, which goes something like this:

"You been climbing at all?" I ask.

"Oh, just climbing out of bed," said with a twinkle in the climber's eyes.

Like everything in life, climbing is fleeting. We won't climb forever, just as we won't live forever. Our climbing experiences mostly vanish just after they are experienced, and then live in the sometimes untrustworthy narrator that is memory. The importance of living in the moment is one of the many lessons that climbing teaches. Because inevitably, someday, it may be a challenge to simply climb out of bed.

A final note I would like to add is that there are more than a few references to illicit drug use in these stories. While I certainly don't promote this behavior, it was how we lived during our younger days, and as a writer, it is my duty to tell the truth. That said, climbing has provided the greatest highs I've ever experienced, and once you've tasted that feeling, no drug can ever compare.

From the mountaintop of maturity it would be easy to look back and wish I hadn't made so many mistakes, taken foolish risks on climbs, or gone after certain women. However, that was how I became the man and writer I am today, and from this vantage point, molded by my mistakes and real life experiences, the view looks pretty good. I hope you enjoy this book.

2 CLIMBING AFTER KEROUAC

There is a time, somewhere between growing up and growing old, a time we all hope to find with others, when you are young in the heart, yet wise enough to understand how fortunate and delicate your situation is.

It was just after a time when life seemed so hopeless and bitter that I moved to Colorado. I was young and desperate to have a foundation to create. What to create? I didn't know. I knew I had to escape the confines of mainstream America though. The details aren't important, but I came to the Gunnison Valley, on the Western Slope, off Highway 50, unhealthy and running on empty. My mind was full of dreams that Jack Kerouac, Neal Cassady, Ken Kesey, Timothy Leary, Tom Wolfe and the Grateful Dead had planted, but were never given the nutrition and light to flourish completely in my naïve, young soul. I had read *On the Road*, the *Electric Kool-Aid Acid Test* and anything I could about the Grateful Dead. The life and the people I wanted to know were there in those pages, there was personal freedom, a different path, so I knew I could find it somewhere in America.

Moving to Gunnison seemed like a horrible idea for the first few months. And it wasn't like I moved there; I ended up there after a summer of following around the bands Phish and Widespread Panic, and chasing a girl that wasn't worth chasing.

The beauty of the mountains, endless wilderness, that's all great, but without a focus, without friends, it's too much openness and freedom. If you are a lonely soul it exposes it like the night shows the moon. I enrolled at Western State as an English student, more out of a survival instinct, than a direction to move my life forward.

Survival instincts carried me through that first cold winter, in a place that is so cold walking outside in the morning with anything less than a down coat, warm hat, gloves and thick pants with long underwear would be crazy.

Come May, school was over, and the magic of living in a mountain town during the summer snuck up on me. I've never been the same. Life had never been so quiet, and all the great novels and poems I'd read manifested themselves in the form of blue skies, suns, moons, trees, birds, rocks and mountain people. Though I aspired to be a writer, I felt no inspiration in the classroom, so I changed my area of studies to Recreation, more freedom and time outside, and set out to learn more about my future profession. I planned climbing trips and purchased a bouldering pad for when I climbed alone, which, in the beginning, was most of the time.

Later, since I'd given up the thought of being a career writer, I began to write. Mostly the poems moved me, moved my fingers to write. It was the wild that I wrote of, mainly poems and occasionally I'd read them to a woman. When you are searching for your identity and swagger, the mountains are easy to find, the mountain women are more difficult to reach.

I had my foundation rooted in the wild with a civilization that encouraged me to create. I never dreamt that in the mountains I would find poets, artists, yogis, writers, musicians, and pseudo-bum athletes. All these creative, underground types loosely united on the basis that most of us struggled to do what we do.

And struggle I would. Personally, my struggles included things like living at a nearby public land area for months on end, having my car break down, and then the winter came, and the authorities hunting me down at my job, "Now why has your car been at this campsite for so long, and what about that marijuana we found in there?"

Or the struggle of having a degree on the wall, but two or three manual labor jobs just to pay the bills and have that time to create. But the struggle can be a blessing, and it feels really great to work hard, and also have that freedom to be a mountain climber or an artist, or simply just be in the high country. As long as you don't give into negativity, due to the struggle.

The struggle, negativity, is much easier to give into when times change, and things get harder. When the rich people move in, rent goes up, the easy college days are over and slowly your friends leave town.

"You know Luke, everyone has their own golden age in the Gunnison Valley," George Sibley told me in the midst of the winter season, the time when negativity has the best chance to flourish in my mind. "It seems there is always someone coming here saying it's the best place they've ever found, and someone leaving saying the place is doomed."

Sibley's an old timer now, forty-year resident of the valley, accomplished writer, and professor at the college. Last year, the mayor of Crested Butte even declared a George Sibley Day. He was young in Crested Butte, in that time-period-age-mentality I was so fascinated with when I stumbled upon The Valley. Funny, he seems so youthful and hopeful still when I sit in his office down at Western State.

Like I said before, my friends the mountain climbers, ski bums, river rats, poets, volunteer radio DJs, etc., finished with college, or whatever mission they were out for in The Valley, are moving on, moving to other mountain towns to follow love, to cities for opportunities, or abroad to interact with different cultures. For me, for the winter anyway, I've got to go, too, to continue the search, to chase new dreams that have been planted by new heroes and writers like Ed Abbey, Martin Luther King Jr. and of course old ones like Kerouac.

So I'll leave off Highway 50 just as I came, and I'll welcome the tears. Knowing they fall because I am grateful that I slept in the dirt so much. I suffered for personal glory in the mountains and made connections with so many genuine people. I'll use that uniquely human trait to be able to remember the good times more than the bad, and recall that maybe just once, perhaps while dancing with all my friends to some live music, that I was on the heels of Cassady and Kerouac.

I'll know one thing for sure about the future of Gunnison, Crested Butte and many other transient mountain towns, that just as myself and many of my comrades are leaving, fresh searchers, young and old, are arriving, and they are going to fall in love with the place and create a new lifestyle for themselves. They might have a guitar on their back, a head full of naïve dreams, or just enough money to buy a new pair of skis, but I know they are destined to find their passions connected with others, to find an energy and mentality lost to mainstream America.

Maybe my hope goes beyond the valley of Colorado I love so much, but it incorporates something I discovered for the first time there. My friend and fellow writer, aspiring vagabond, snowboarder, and musician Greg Pettys, writes in his essay *Things Change, the Mountains are Here Forever,* "As long as there are mountains, I have a home; as long as there are open spaces where a soul can connect with its creator; as long as there is beauty, uncertainty and adventure, I will have a home."

A version of this story was originally published in the Crested Butte Magazine, Summer 2006.

3 UNTITLED, INSPIRED BY HARTMAN ROCKS

Been so long since me and the fire talked, so long, even without words the fire speaks to me, so friendly, so different. So quickly it burns the wood, burns it away, to ash, ashes of gray stay not so long. Flowing but not saying anything, teaching. Am I learning? Am I writing because I am wise? Should I burn this poem? Nah, keep it rollin' like a doobie, smoked all the way through. Coyote howls, so important is the coyote to the land. Heard but not seen. Seen to the land, for sure and seen by those it is meant to. Sage smells so good. I write, I write to you, you dig? Dig down deep, sometimes we must to accomplish success and live close to our dreams. What do you dream of? I dream of my friends on alone nights like these. I dream of only being alone, and not lonely. I dream of a long life in Colorado. Throw another log on the fire, make the night last a little longer. Not wanting it to last forever and not wanting it to burn out. But we all will burn out and fade away, someday just like my headlamp and the campfire. Pop, says the fire and not much longer before it fades away. Trying to live in that moment, and finding that to be the biggest challenge of my life.

A version of this poem was originally published in The Gunnison Valley Journal, fourth edition.

4 WIDE EYES, HIGH TIMES AND HARD TIMES, A STORY OF CLIMBING WITH MARK GRUNDON

Say a prayer for those you love and everyone else. That's what I've written on my sleeping pad, and the last words I read before going to bed. The first person I pray for lately is my friend Mark Grundon. Mark is twenty two years old and has cancer, or hopefully, by now, had cancer.

I can vividly remember the first time I saw Mark on the campus of Western State College in Gunnison, Colorado. He was leaving a class and I was going to one. I was admiring the fresh new faces on campus (checking out women). Somehow Mark stood out from the crowd with his wild appearance: six foot two, matted dreadlocks and wild blue eyes.

Through the college's search and rescue team, a fine group that is considered the best of its kind in the country, that also offered camaraderie in abundance, we met and became acquaintances.

I can remember the first time I saw him, but in the next couple of years, maybe due to all the college parties, I don't remember how much we hung out. But we were both climbers and passionate about it. Mark is the most motivated climber I've ever met. Like many college students, my passion surpassed my motivation to actually do something, so Mark was an ideal friend and climbing partner.

When Mark and I first started climbing together he was working for the National Park Service, waking early, around six and getting off around dinnertime. Mark would motivate me to show him some obscure routes in a nearby canyon. We'd climb till dark and immediately, when the day was over, he'd be trying to hook me into more climbing plans, likely the next day after his long shift. This is Mark Grundon, an honest hardworking American, wide eyed, packing as much life into each and every day as possible.

The climbing adventures would continue, as would the parties and growing and learning as climbing partners, and more importantly, as friends. The winters around Gunnison are cold and seem to last forever (forever-ever), if you don't keep yourself mentally and physically occupied.

I was never prepared for winter, and the five winters I went through while going to college there, I suffered through each one. I'd hibernate and lose track of Mark. Mark, of course, didn't sink into the denial of winter I had. He got himself a job at the nearby Monarch ski area, this while maintaining a near perfect GPA at Western State, with a double major in Environmental Studies and Recreation.

His first winter, Mark was skiing up Monarch and fell, lacerating his liver. He was flown out by helicopter to Denver. They stitched up his liver and part of it was removed. I found this out the following season at a party at his house. Mark was never the guy who partied his college away. Plus, he couldn't abuse his liver with alcohol like the rest of us. So while we'd take over his house, the only one we knew of in town with a hot tub (girls would always get naked in a hot tub), Mark would mostly be studying in his room maintaining that nearly perfect GPA, keeping his healthy perspective on life while the rest of us went on partying, acting like we'd be young forever.

Occasionally, Mark would party, and I'd be drunk, trying to get him to drink. I'm sure I was obnoxious and one night I was giving Mark an unusually hard time about not boozing. My ladyfriend got upset with me about that, and then Mark would start to tease me about something, usually the girl, and we'd break out into a wrestling match.

So our friendship was born and molded by rock climbing, partying and some good natured teasing. Another winter would come around, and by then I knew I had to do something to remain sane and avoid sinking into the dark depression of winter. The only thing I could come up with was to continue climbing. Sure there was the college climbing gym, but pulling on plastic can only build up physical strength. My mental health was what worried me. School kept me active as well, and girls would come and go. But I needed to climb, outside.

My solution to combat the inevitable seasonal depression, cabin fever, whatever you want to call it, had one major problem. We were living in a place often referred to as The Coldest City in the Lower 48. Truth be told though, it's not really a city, or technically the coldest, but it's a relatively fair assessment. It's not uncommon to wake up in the dead of winter in Gunnison to find it's negative twenty out, or even colder. I believe it's the combination of the high altitude, an open valley and the close proximity to the Blue Mesa Reservoir. Either way, it will chill you to the bone, and it comes as no surprise that less than ten thousand people live there year round. Some say there are more elk and deer than people in the region. Two and a half hours to the west, though, is a red rock sandstone desert at lower altitude, with some great climbing.

We could wake up at seven, down a quick breakfast and coffee and be climbing in forty degree temps by ten o'clock. By noon, I'd forget I lived in such a cold place, and my spirit would be a little warmer, which was exactly what my cold, hardened soul needed. But who could I convince that driving five hours a day in the winter for a few hours of climbing was a good idea?

The first trip Mark and I made together was the worst. It was November, the start of the dreaded winter. It was one of those rare days when Escalante Canyon wasn't a desert paradise, in fact it was snowing off and on with a wicked wind brewing. By the time we starting climbing, the wind was whipping and making us suffer.

Escalante is a quiet place where man's influence is minimal. There are some cows, a river, and lots of dirt and rock. Up to the wall, where we would climb, there was no distinguished trail. We just wandered up the red dirt through juniper trees, and Mormon tea bushes, a green broom like, shrub with jointed stems. Ahead, red rock walls, a couple hundred feet tall, with cracks to climb.

Despite the fact that it was snowing and the wind was whipping, Mark was still psyched to climb. Without his motivation, I would have just given up and gotten stoned. He even wanted the lead. I agreed, knowing the climb we were preparing to do would work him good, but how long could it take?

The climb we were about to get on isn't described in any guidebook; therefore, I cannot provide a name. Mark began up a perfect hand crack, which had no other features other than the split in the rock. He was vaguely familiar with this technique of climbing those cracks, quite different than our backyard climbs in Gunnison, but he slowly struggled up the wall. I've been trying for years to pen the joys and philosophies of climbing as it can relate to normal everyday life. My experiences with Mark this day slowly logged themselves in my brain. Looking up at Mark, it became clear this climb was much more than just a challenge. He lacked the training in technique, and prior experience to know how to do it. Yet somehow, inch by inch, in the cold and intermittent snow, he was reaching the top, jamming his hands and feet into the crack, accepting the pain of it.

He used some techniques modern purist climbers might call cheating, resting on his protection pieces wedged in the crack, but with no one but myself and God watching, how could it be called cheating?

Two men suffering in the wilderness. Mark in the physical realm, managing his way up the steep red rock wall. I was suffering in the mental realm, on the ground belaying, tending the rope, challenged by patience for being there for your friend. I did my best to send nothing but encouraging words up. Mark struggled on. The time came when I'd usually lose my patience, cursing myself for bringing a less experienced climber along and letting him lead. But there was something about his determination that kept me from anger.

It was cold, it was November and I wasn't depressed. Something about fresh air, wind, rock, and dirt that keep one from depression, a recipe that should be prescribed in moderate doses, to all who are sad.

I was paying the dues for a climbing friendship that would grow and blossom and we were suffering together in the Colorado red rock wilderness. Though we'd been hanging out for years, it was a beginning. The start of our adventures in desert climbing. The start of being brothers of the rock and the road, away from home, away from the college parties, taking down some of the walls we all put up in civilization, to where we were just two young men, excited about life and willing to suffer to climb them walls.

We would make about thirty more trips to Escalante Canyon, our new winter climbing home, over the next couple of years. Mark was as fun to drive in the car with, as he was to climb with. He was what mountain folk would call always psyched. He had a childlike lust for life. I was an old, tired soul in need of a friend like Mark. He could get excited for the silliest of things, and his excitement was infectious.

The drive to Escalante is long for a day trip, so he would designate landmarks as we drove from Gunnison, through the towns of Montrose and Delta to Escalante. The more he tried to create landmarks, the weirder they became. It started with the Giant Boob, a Department of Transportation structure halfway to Montrose, that modestly resembled a fake boob, nipple and all.

With pure excitement and a manic energy he would yell, "Giant Boooob," each time we passed the structure. Just outside of Delta, headed west, we discovered a yard with odd alien lawn ornaments, a monster truck on top of a crashed car and even a boat on a pole.

Mark was fun and he quickly improved at wrestling the sandstone crack climbs. One semester, Mark and I had the dream schedule at Western State, modeled after many Crested Butte skiers: class on Monday, Wednesday, and Friday, with Tuesdays and Thursdays off. So of course we'd go to Escalante. My obligations were minimal: a part time dishwashing job and two courses at the college. Mark however, no slacker, was ski patrolling at Monarch, taking more than a full school schedule, as well as working on his Emergency Medical Technician (EMT) certification.

Escalante Tuesdays were the days. Mark provided the motivation to leave early, and I would provide the avocado and cheese sandwiches. We'd usually take his little Hyundai, only ten bucks in gas, there and back. And of course, there would be holidays, and he would be ready to climb on those days too. We'd climbed so many of the cracks within our ability level there by then, so we began to search for the Holy Grail of routes to climbers, untouched, unclimbed ones. The climbing in Escalante had been going on since the seventies, so most of the obvious safe cracks have been done. The leftovers from the golden age of climbing in the west were typically littered with some loose rock, but some were desirable. If your mindset was like ours, a strong desire for a first ascent, a little loose rock, or even a lot, wouldn't deter you.

On the Martin Luther King Jr. holiday of 2003, we found ourselves looking up at an unclimbed route, obvious that no human had ever climbed it because of the many loose blocks in the first fifteen feet of the pitch. One feature, similar looking to a snow bollard, a ball of rock a few square feet around, hovered above us, destined to meet with the ground as soon as we got up to it and knocked it off. Though it was clearly a dangerous climb, both of us wanted our hands on it.

We eyed the line, with a hint of competition, like we were both after the same woman. Since I had more experience, and karma wise

19

I'd spent lots of time belaying Mark, it was agreed that I would lead. I didn't have the warrior like mental focus needed for steep, difficult climbing, and each move was a battle, made more difficult because of the unstable nature of the rock. I would reach up for a hold, and it would crumble away. When I'd step down with my feet, the same thing would happen. Any time I found a hold to move up on, I'd be afraid it would crumble and send me back tumbling to the ground. After ten feet of groveling through loose rock, I arrived at a ledge five feet left of the bollard feature.

Once I arrived at the ledge, I was too chicken to traverse on my feet, so I simply crawled across it on my belly, as it was perfectly featured to do so. The scene was comical, but frightful at the time. Funny how climbing is sometimes the most joyous thing in the world, while other times it is a nightmare. I must've looked like a fool to Mark, but he stood there belaying patiently. I got to the bollard feature and karate kicked it off the wall, sending the three foot tall ball of rock just beside Mark. Finally, I'd reached the perfect crack. I used the same techniques Mark did the year before, weighting the protection I'd placed in the rock, while knocking down loose rocks trying to miss Mark. At a snail's pace, some say rock climbing can be one of the slowest forms of human movement, I eventually finished the climb.

Mark faced what I had with seeming ease. Moves that I had struggled with, he performed with delicate execution. I was witnessing the student growing closer to the teacher in ability. In climbing, all are equal, regardless what the ego says. I was not envious of Mark, his passion was shared. Quickly, Mark was figuring out the techniques to climb these desert cracks, and he reached my perch with grace. We called the climb, Living The Dream, to commemorate Dr. King, and to reflect the dream lives we'd been living that winter.

The following week, we were back, hungry for another first ascent experience. While I was bolting the anchors on Living The

Dream, Mark had discovered a perfect crack, right around the corner, that looked like it had never been climbed. Since I got to lead the previous week, Mark would get the sharp end this time. Mark started up the stunning crack, split in a corner, like an open book, jamming his fingers and toe tips in the crack, placing the mechanical cams as he went. Forty feet up, I heard some mumbling fearful chatter followed by an, "Oh shit."

Before I even had a chance to think, Mark had fallen thirty plus feet, upside down. The rope had gotten caught around his foot, and he was now looking me directly in the eyes, hovering a few feet from the ground. A piece had popped from the crack, the rope stretched a little, but luckily his second piece held. If not he would have landed on the ground headfirst. For a second, I saw Mark more wide eyed than ever, and we went through some climber dialogue.

"Are you okay?"

"Yeah."

"Holy shit dude."

"I know."

My friend could have just died, had things gone slightly differently. If he had landed directly on his head, I'd be in charge of leading a rescue, and with no one around, it might take hours to get him to help. But, he was fine, and our focus would have to turn back to the climb.

What to do now? Our gear was placed in the inch wide crack above us. All of it added up to a couple hundred dollars. We couldn't just walk away. One of us would have to complete the seventy foot climb. The crack hadn't exactly been friendly to Mark, but I geared up, and used the most conservative techniques I knew to climb a rock. I quickly saw why Mark had been spit out of the crack, green lichen grew on the edges, and the climb was perfectly vertical. We still thought it had never been climbed before. As I reached the place of his fall, I was resting on the gear. I inched to the top of the climb and disappointingly there was an anchor, a bogus sketchy chockstone at that, evidence we were not the first to climb the thing. But we were both alive and uninjured, and deemed the day a success. And we had a story to tell when we got back to Gunnison.

As always, winter turns to spring, the cold is forgotten, and the seed of dreams planted turns to reality. Eventually Mark and I were climbing at the same level. Being a desert climber means little in the grand scheme of things, and in a technical sense it basically means you've figured out how to jam your limbs into a variety of crack sizes. In your heart, it means a lot more. Climbing changes lives. Over a season in the desert, I learned to trust Mark with my life on the end of the rope, and together we spent many days in the car and in the desert growing.

The summer following our winter breakthrough, as school was done, Mark was off on another adventure to Alaska, spending his summer guiding helicopter/glacier travel adventures. In the fall, when school started back up, I was living out of my truck, standard for any climber at some point in their lives. Mark invited me to park the truck outside of his newly rented home. It's a situation many a climber has dreamed of, living for free, surrounded by friends, and having all the luxuries of a modern home. I stayed, living out of the truck for a few months until it really got cold.

Just before the cold set in, we planned a climbing weekend, starting with the nearby Black Canyon, followed by a day in Escalante. The Black in November is always a gamble. There was always the chance that we could be caught in a storm a thousand feet up on those intimidating granite walls.

And how to describe The Black? It has the tallest wall in Colorado, the twenty three hundred foot Painted Wall; a crumbly thing with pink pegmatite strokes that run diagonal across it. Driving towards the canyon rim, the landscape looks flat. Park the car at the primitive campground at the North Rim, where most of the climbing is done, hike a couple hundred yards, and there is the void. See the guardrail, stop and look down two thousand feet, with the ever moving Gunnison River roaring below. People have jumped off and committed suicide right there. Climbers have been on the wall and discovered body parts. I've heard that the Natives, the Utes, believed the place was haunted. Without a guardrail, it was probably spookier. The first time I walked up on that guardrail, I started to believe in evil spirits, and my stomach sunk deep down. But there is an equally empowering positive energy that one can access on the sheer gray walls, inching upward to the rim.

That morning in The Black, we were one of just two climbing parties, and the sky didn't indicate there was a storm coming in. Even though winter was in the air, I was with Mark and he was psyched. I had done the climb once before, The Journey Home, named after an Edward Abbey book, with a most exciting initial section of the climb (long run out without gear for falls). We approached the climb, and stared up at the beginning of our vertical world for the day. I felt calm knowing Mark would be leading the first dangerous section. He climbed off, set a piece of protection, and then embarked on a long section without any pro for falls, not that difficult of moves, but sure to send all the adrenaline in one's brain tingling down the body. I let out rope, and watched Mark weave his body along small edges on the dark gray rock, with swirls of pink and lighter tones of gray. The rope hung from his harness, mostly useless for now, as he danced his way up the wall.

At one point, he knocked down a small chunk of rock, but managed to stay on. It was a good thing too. Had he fallen, it would have been to where I was standing twenty feet below. He was simply in a position where he couldn't fall, and he didn't. He climbed higher and secured good gear, a relief for both of us. The rest of the climb went smooth; each time we'd set out and climb a full rope length, two hundred feet.

On my leads, I remember staring off into the never ending vastness of the canyon, it goes on for something like fifty miles, feeling tiny and empty, and then eventually Mark would draw nearer. I'd notice those wide eyes, and soon after that, we were on the perch together, a ledge just enough to put our feet on, dangling almost a thousand feet above the canyon floor, just two people, but a closeness and enthusiasm that I've rarely found except when I was in the wilderness with a friend. And Mark was (is) the best of friends, and full of the purest energy and enthusiasm.

The energy of climbing in the wilderness led us onward to the top of the wall, a thousand plus feet above where we began. Three other friends, from Western State, who had been the only other climbers in the canyon, were there to meet us with cold beers, a rare treat. Usually when we top out, there's no one there or some curious sightseers, asking questions like, "ya'll been climbing down there?" We were the only people there in the vast park, no surprise; we were on the heels of old man winter. The sun left us, and we cooked a humble meal in the cold night and then left the canyon for the season, for another favorite, where we always go when things get too cold, Escalante Canyon.

Escalante, no secret, no surprise we'd learned many lessons, survived the falls, and now it was an old friend. There was little, if any, mystery of what to do when we woke up. We ate some food and hiked up the hillside to a red rock sandstone crag. Once again it felt right to be in the desert. We would spend all day climbing different cracks.

In the Black Canyon, we picked up The Benson, a particularly funny young man from Gunnison. The Benson added an essential element to the day, humor, there's never too much. Mark once described him as a teddy bear. As we were laughing, climbing, laughing, climbing, just as fast as the autumn fades to winter, the sun steadily leaves the day. Usually as the day is ending I lose my energy, but Mark sees the setting sun as an opportunity, for more life, for one more climb. I've learned I better bring a headlamp if I'm climbing with Mark, and we walked down the hillside, well after the sun had set.

The winter soon came upon us, but by now we were too good of friends to just lose track of one another. Basically we were family now. One morning after a snowy weekend, I stopped by Mark's house to say hello.

"How was the ice climbing this weekend?" I asked. They'd been climbing near Silverton, Colorado, that weekend, a couple hours southwest of Gunnison.

"Not so good, we had an accident," he told me somberly with a look of despair in his eyes.

Mark and his roommate Scott Borden, and Steve Nigro, another climbing friend, had gotten hit by an avalanche, while they were well into the climb. Steve, who was leading, fell over two hundred feet to the base of the climb, while Mark and Scott were nearly ripped from their anchor from the force of the avalanche. They all could have died. They immediately went into rescue mode, and got help for Steve. He was rushed to the hospital in Montrose and spent the night there. Quickly, we made plans to visit Steve that afternoon.

For the first time ever in the winter, we were heading west towards Montrose, not for the pleasure of climbing, but to visit an injured friend. We arrived in the evening to see Steve in a hospital bed, tired and injured, but alert and in good spirits. He was the reality of what could happen to you while climbing. I didn't know what to say. There wasn't really much we could do. We gave him some food, and told him we admired him. Time was the only thing that would heal the wounds, which included injuries to the discs in his back and a broken sternum. We left, he needed rest, but I knew from surviving that kind of fall, that his body was as strong as steel, his spirit as strong as any other human's I'd known.

Winter went on. Slow as winter does, as did the sadness that comes with it. Steve was healing slowly. Mark and Scott were mentally recovering, too. But life is sometimes like the avalanche; the hard times just keep coming down. I was at work, washing dishes in Crested Butte, when I received a phone call from Mark with the news. He'd been diagnosed with testicular cancer. He immediately needed a surgery to remove his testicle, and would have to leave in two days to Vermont, where he grew up. I didn't know what to say, and I didn't know what to do.

Mark's surgery in Vermont was successful, and soon after, he returned to Colorado for radiation treatment and his final semester at Western State. Mark faced this challenge with the same determination and courage I had witnessed in his climbing. Never did he submit to negativity.

His routine now didn't leave him a minute of free time. He had six weeks of radiation treatment to do in Grand Junction, which meant getting up at 6:00 a.m., driving to Junction to do his treatment, and then driving back to Gunnison for school. This was what he had to do. Certain days he would challenge himself a little more. Many days he'd get zapped (his slang for radiation), and then head over to Escalante Canyon for a quick climb. Typically, he would climb more than whoever was along for the adventure. More than one person reported to me that Mark out climbed them, this from a guy being treated for cancer.

At first he was nauseous and couldn't eat. He lost ten pounds. The medicine he received, along with numerous other pills of God knows what, didn't help. The doctor gave him weed, or as they call it marinol, synthetic marijuana pills. It worked. Immediately, his appetite returned. Once his friends found out the marinol was helping, they began to offer all forms of marijuana products. One group of friends concocted some ganja peanut butter (peanut butter with weed in it). Mark, unlike many college students in Gunnison, didn't care to smoke pot, so the effect was just like someone getting stoned for the first time.

One night after he had sampled some of the peanut butter, I stopped by the house to find him lying in the middle of his kitchen floor, laughing hysterically. Indeed, the unimaginable stress of being a full time college senior, while undergoing radiation treatment for cancer hadn't gotten to his sense of humor.

Mark, already a respected member of the Gunnison community, was now a hero. At the college, a professor organized a ride system so that Mark would never have to ride alone. I went with him several times. Waking up at six in the morning was rough, how did he do this day after day?

At the cancer treatment center, they invited us to go back in the radiation room, with that big machine above Mark's body to administer the radiation. It was freaky, and even more disturbing they had to put his privates in a weird metal cup. The doctor's assistants explained the whole process, and we watched via a television outside the radiation room. This, day after day, and Mark never lost his cool. The only thing that upset him was the one cookie limit in the lobby, "These people are going through cancer, can't they have more than one damn cookie," he'd say.

On the drive back that day we were talking about our usual topics: girls, parties, climbing, politics, the environment and girls. Scott, who was along for this trip, had been spending some time with a lady, and Mark started asking him about it, "So how did it go last night?"

Scott wasn't interested in talking about it. "Not so good," he said after a little prodding.

"Well, what happened?" Mark asked.

"Ummmm, I don't really want to talk about it," Scott said.

"Dude, you just saw my balls in a metal cup," Mark added.

And, Scott told his story.

Over the course of his radiation treatment, Mark had earned my admiration and respect, and the same was true for many others. After the treatment was completed, there was a big party in his little house. His parents flew in from Vermont, and Mark did the MC Hammer dance like a wild man. It was an essential celebration, cancer, radiation, five hours of driving every weekday, none of it defeated his spirit.

And continue on he did. He went back to ski patrolling at Monarch, back to climbing (he never stopped) and started planning for another adventurous summer. Sure enough, he scored an opportunity to be a summer guide on Mt. Shasta in California, which would be an internship to complete his Recreation degree.

Mark had to try out for his position to be a mountain guide, so in his usual cramming as much life into every moment style, he did this just before his graduation ceremony at Western State. I just happened to be a few hours north in Bend, Oregon, on a climbing trip, so it worked out perfectly that we could drive back together.

I rolled into Mt. Shasta City in the afternoon. It was foggy, and the mountain could not be seen. I found Mark's new house for the summer. He got the job and had spent the weekend on the mountain and partying like climbers do. "I'm so tired of talking about climbing," he told me. "It's been a nonstop spray fest."

Indeed climbing is something that's better to do and just keep quiet about it, which is easier to write than to do. So we packed up my truck with Mark's climbing gear and headed east, back home.

Mark told me about his future fellow employees and the crystal people that come to Mt. Shasta to charge their crystals, as it is one of the sacred seven summits. He told me about the breast cancer fundraiser that they did on Mt. Shasta. I'd been doing some solo traveling on the trip, and it didn't bother me at all that Mark was talking nonstop. The constant presence of a true friend is no doubt appreciated more after solitude. We drove through the forests of Northern California which took us to Nevada. Poor, lonely Nevada, full of lifeless desert and casinos; Mark went on talking, and we made stops for gas and coffee.

The nighttime in Nevada, forever of nothing, but the white and yellow lines, and the truck powering down the highway. Then bright, bright, blinking lights on the horizon, an insanity supported by the gamblers. In Reno, there was no urge to stop. Gambling could be fun, but the prospect that we might have time to climb in the Utah desert called us. Nighttime driving meant one of us would sleep, while the other would put as much coffee in his system as possible. Mark actually stopped talking for a little bit. What he was talking about is gone to the past, but set to the rhythm of the road, and the hip-hop that played on the radio.

We were both up at sunrise, as Nevada ended, one last big casino of course, on the state's edge. Then Utah began and past the great lake, Salt Lake City came into the horizon. Oh, America and its duality. Nevada, home of prostitution and gambling, fades into Utah, home of the Mormons, of young adventurers like us, and I'm sure a lot of other kinds of folk too. Ah, to be young, low on sleep, high on caffeine, rolling into a city with no attachments, no real plan, the sun coming up, the city people getting going, the semi trucks on their endless journey heading out of town and into town. We arrived at the destination, and we had a friend in Salt Lake, an old college buddy, and we found his house so we could pass out.

As we show up on Adam Lawton's doorstep, he was just getting ready to rise for grad school, "You guys can sleep as long as you want. I've got to go to class. I'll be back in the afternoon."

We slept for a couple of hours and woke to the most horrible smell of paint drying with none of the windows open for ventilation. Someone was painting the damn bathroom. Why did it have to be the morning we arrived? Though there was nothing we wanted more than sleep, there was no hope for it with the toxic state of Adam's studio. We stumbled out on the streets of Salt Lake City.

Wandering across the city over to a market, what do we hear but "Let's get wild," an old college phrase that we used to say when we got excited. I looked back, and walking down the street was Adam. Goofy and intelligent, one of our people, with his wild blond hair flowing in all directions he proclaims, "We should go to this Tibetan buffet over by my house."

Fed and then caffeinated, Mark and I make a quick trip to the library to get information about a climb and then head south to Moab, our destination for the evening. Driving on so little sleep, I'm irritable, but more caffeine takes care of that. Mark and I barely talk, our brains are foggy, we're leaving a city, and aren't all cities a bit confusing after living in small towns for so long?

Though we don't talk, I wonder what he thinks, and he seems to communicate with those wild blue eyes. Is he scared of death after so many close encounters with it? But those eyes say to me, I've lived and died a hundred times before.

Driving across the United States, we'd seen the forests of Northern California to the desert of Nevada, and now we crossed from Salt Lake City headed south, desolate and lonely, to the red rock desert of Moab, the real thing, man. The real thing if you're a dreamer, an outdoorsman, a climber, like us. If you've read *Desert Solitaire* by Ed Abbey, and he planted dreams in your head of adventure in the forms of rock towers, red dirt, lone ravens, cactus, juniper trees and blue, so blue, skies.

Our destination is Castle Valley, home of the prettiest rock towers I've seen, some four hundred feet tall, and very climbable. We set up camp, which only means throwing our sleeping pads and bags in the dirt and getting some food in our guts. Mark wants to wake up before sunrise to get an early start, and who am I to argue?

Motivation for that desert high gets us up way early. The landscape we can't see it yet, it's still dark, but we know it's there because we've been here before. We don't hear much noise from the ten some climbers camping nearby. There is competition for these climbs, the gems of Castle Valley. It may have been what Abbey feared, the inevitable popularity and population of the red rock desert, but it's really no big deal. We just have to get up before they do.

We hike up to the Rectory, the first tower we plan to climb for the day. The sunlight replaces the headlamp and the towers, along with the nearby La Sal Mountains to the southwest are unveiled. Our legs are well conditioned. I've been on a three week climbing trip, and Mark, he's always in good shape. Hiking is a pleasure when you're prepared, and the suffering is little to none. The workout feels divine and puts our minds exactly in the moment. We find the base of the Rectory. Castleton is just behind us, a perfectly square four hundred foot tower.

Our objective in front of us is a four hundred foot series of cracks up red rock sandstone. The tower itself is slender. It is long, three hundred feet wide or so, and juts into the blue sky. On the boulders above the red dirt, we organize our climbing gear.

I take the lead first, jamming hands in the crack, breathe, jam, feet (bam), breathe, jam, breathe, a few times over for a hundred and fifty feet. What a way to wake up. Did we eat breakfast? I'm sure we did, but I don't remember what. I hope that I'll forever remember hanging on above the void, above my belayer Mark, striving to get higher and higher. Mark comes up to my perch, a nice little ledge, and sets off for harder climbing above, perfect style, the reward for our lonely days in Escalante. Not so lonely here, I look back and there are climbers approaching up the hills we climbed a couple hours before. It feels so divine to climb in good style, hell, good style or reckless struggle, look around and you'll have a view to remember. Red rock is everywhere. Of course, a few lone ravens are up and about. In the distance is a winery, which adds welcome greenery to the surroundings.

I clean Mark's pitch, yanking the gear out while still hanging on. And then there we are, a hundred feet below the summit, still early as hell. Mark is rather excited and talkative. He's here in his element, late spring in the wild desert, always a sense of reward for those who endured a cold winter. How good does it feel for a guy that spent his winter treating cancer in a hospital? Well I can tell you he was psyched and the excitement was building in his chatter. The guy likes to talk, loves to get excited.

We don't hang out long, and soon I'm leading off for the summit pitch. Just because you're near the top, doesn't mean it's over. Some sandy, exciting climbing begins the pitch. The sand makes me question my foundation; each foothold seems a little insecure. In the moment, at least I'm trying to be, Mark is still talking a mile a minute. I try to focus on the climbing. Mark is still jabbering about God knows what. The morning has packed in so much adrenaline, workout and joy. Quickly, I am entering a fearful state, and I need to concentrate as much as I can, "Will you shut up," I yell to Mark.

He doesn't take offense because he knows the process my brain is going through. We are brothers of climbing. I'm inching up, the sandiness disappears, the quality of rock perfect again, the climbing harder and harder still, but protected by bolts, which all I have to do is clip 'em with a carabineer. And there I am. Later there we are on the summit, and it's still before noon. "Let's get in another tower," he says.

I was waiting for him to say it, and it's decided. We rappel back to the ground. Our next objective is just around the bend, a route called the Honeymoon Chimney on the Priest formation. We hike over and have a granola bar lunch. We're a little tired. Mark decides to do something about it and finds a good place to stand on his head, a yogic way of revitalizing energy.

It's Mark's lead. He starts to wiggle himself in the chimney. With chimney climbing, you just put your whole body in the crack. Physically demanding, and mentally too, when the protection for falls is limited. He's got a rock in the back of the crack slung with some webbing, clips a mediocre bolt, but doesn't have it. Grunting Grundon, struggling and wiggling, not much progress, after a half an hour, "I don't have it. Do you want to try it?"

"Well, hell no, if you can't get it," I felt good enough. The desert was alive within me, or at least I had that high. I know that feeling and it's much better than exhaustion. Our day has been good enough. There's no one keeping score in rock climbing.

It's a little past noon. We hike back down as the hills wind through red rocks and red dirt. The clouds are rolling in a little. We feel good. I feel perfectly content with The Rectory being the final climb of the road trip. Should we go back to Moab for lunch? It's out of the way, but how good is a prepared meal when you've been eating camping meals? So good, but not good enough to use that much gas, that much time to go out of the way. Our way is east, back to Colorado, back to Gunnison. River Road, east, soon its I-70, soon enough Grand Junction; food, food, what else would we think of?

Once he's energized with a modest meal, Mark starts talking of more climbing for the day. I go along with the plan for a bit, but the comforts of home have already entered my mind. I can try, but I usually can't keep up with Mark. He's disappointed I don't want to get a couple of afternoon climbs in Escalante. I feel guilty and start to come up with excuses. There we are in Grand Junction, the center of our desert experiences; Mark always ready for more living, more climbing.

We drive in on Highway 50, which takes us home. Mark is about to graduate in a week. Immediately, he's got a lot on his plate, but he's used to it. He graduates, with honors, cum laude I think they call it. His parents, Cheryl and Steve, come back to town, and he takes them up a desert tower in Colorado National Monument, near Junction. He's back in Gunnison for a day or two, then destined for California, to Yosemite for some big-wall climbing, up to Mt. Shasta for some guide training, back to Yosemite then to Colorado for a stop in Gunnison, then up to Estes Park for an eight day American Mountain Guides Association (AMGA) training course.

After California and another drive across the west, he stops at our house for some rest. He tells some stories, of a flood in Yosemite and climbing El Capitan with a random English guy he'd met in Camp 4, the historic campsite in the Yosemite. "Yeah we were four pitches from the top and my partner had to catch a flight back to Europe the next day. So we rappelled two thousand feet back to the ground."

No sense of failure in his eyes or words, though. A few hours at the house, a nap, and he's gone to Estes Park. Eight days for his AMGA course and the stories don't end. Most of his climbing gear has been stolen, and that is just the start. When he arrives back in Gunnison, he calls me, "My cancer has come back."

He found out while in Estes Park, from tests done a few weeks prior. My heart sinks. I must be with my friend. I'm homeless again, so we meet at a three bedroom apartment where five, maybe six friends are living. He tells me of his experiences with the AMGA course, and getting his gear stolen. His spirit not yet broken, if it isn't by now, I know it never will be.

The next day before leaving, he's decided to cut his hair off, "It would fall off in chemotherapy anyways," he told us. He leaves it half cut is some wild fashion, which makes all of us laugh at dinner that night at the new hip restaurant in Gunnison, called Bowlz. "Man, just when Gunnison gets cool I have to leave," he joked.

We all can forget, Mark too hopefully, if even for just a moment, that he has cancer and just enjoy each other's company. The restaurant had just opened, it took hours to get our food, but that was just fine. So we all laughed, had a couple beers and didn't talk of climbing once, which Mark and I agreed we had been doing too much of over the years. That night he even found a friend, Aaron, to drive back to Vermont with him, where he'd be doing the chemo, opposite of where he'd planned to be, California.

During his summer of chemotherapy, I talked to him several times, not often enough, but each time we talked I'd get nothing but positive energy, positive thoughts. He missed it so badly up here in the high country, God's country. He seemed to never want to end the phone conversations. We'd talk for hours. He was doing the treatment in Burlington, which he called Girlington. Girls are indeed essential for a young man to have around, but I knew he just wanted to be in the mountains.

In the summer, at work watching TV during my shift meal, we'd watch the Tour de France, with the great cyclist Lance Armstrong, now a testicular cancer survivor. Lance seemed to have the same hope and energy flowing through his veins that Mark did, and everyday my belief that Mark too would be a cancer survivor grew. Summers go so fast when they are preceded and followed by months and months of snow and cold. I doubt the summer went fast for Mark, though.

Times are so great now in my life, but they can't last forever. When they get harder, and things might seem overwhelming, I'll think of Mark Grundon, a climber, Mark Grundon, a young man wise beyond his years. When times get hard, I'll think of Mark Grundon, who knows hard times.

Mark finished successful chemotherapy treatment in 2005. He is now a climbing guide in Yosemite, California and El Potrero Chico, Mexico. A shorter version of this story was originally published in the Mountain Gazette.

5 THE WAY OF THE COUCH SURFER

Couch surfing, like the sport with the board, requires a balance and skills that are learned with practice over time. An expert couch surfer is not only welcome by her host, but is also wanted. A poor one is a burden and is rid of as soon as possible.

I'm thinking you're either with me on the board ready to ride this wave, or you're lost in the water. My parents were confused, too, when I introduced couch surfing to them. They're your typical home owning, old fashioned, Midwest parents. In the mainstream America they live in, couch surfing is a novelty, a conversation piece about wild mountain people. In the Gunnison Valley, Colorado it is a system, a way of living, something going on at all times, in someone's house.

The classic Gunny Valley surfer is a transient. Fred claims Crested Butte as home, even has a Post Office Box, but truthfully is more of a modern gypsy than a resident. He just spent the winter in Hawaii, a year in Nicaragua, some time back home and now wants to settle down in CB for the summertime. Problem is he's broke, but he has friends who have a house. They understand his situation, and talking to him at night is way more entertaining than television. Fred is now staying there. He is a bona fide couch surfer.

Christine is another ideal example of the twenty something adventurer that just moved back to CB. She spent the winter on ski patrol on Mt. Crested Butte. Spring started off in Indian Creek, Utah, for a month of rock climbing, soaking in the warm weather before guiding a successful trip up Denali, the continent's highest peak in Alaska. She's back in town, and multiple friends have offered free shelter at their houses.

Both Fred and Christine know the way of the successful couch surfer. They wash dishes and clean up after themselves. They cook dinner for their hosts. Both know when to be there, and are careful to be aware when to leave, most importantly when their hosts have romantic situations going down. Christine writes nice notes and occasionally includes a few dollars. Fred buys small gifts and even puts chocolates on his host's pillow. These are people you'll never want to leave, but of course they will, off on more adventures to places like Mexico, Europe, California, Africa or Thailand with the change of the seasons.

The Guy on the Couch is at the other end of the spectrum. The Guy has wandered out to Colorado to get away from his parents. He's got a buddy that just moved to Gunnison. On a whim, he's come to town, surprising his friend. The Guy doesn't clean up after himself. He hasn't announced his intentions of how long he's staying, and rarely leaves the couch, except for when he goes out to the bar. He's annoyed all the roommates, and his friend is figuring out how to send him packing back home.

Luckily, The Guy on the Couch is a rarity. The system seems to weed out people like this quickly through networking. The depth of networking can be seen on the web at couchsurfing.com, which has opportunities to connect with people from over two hundred countries, from Afghanistan to Zimbabwe, who will let you stay at their place. The site, in its own words is, "a worldwide network for making connections between travelers and the local communities they visit."

One can log on and find a place to stay where she or he is traveling, or offer a place for travelers coming to their area. There is a section to rate those who do come and visit. Safety tips for female travelers are also available.

Couch surfing also includes a realm beyond just staying on the couch. Given the creative nature of the endeavor, one can imagine the possibilities. Personally, I find couches too uncomfortable to actually sleep on. I usually stay on the floor, and for a while this summer, I had a tent set up in a friend's front yard. This past winter my friend Mark Grundon, a big wall rock climber, had one of those hanging tents used for staying overnight on giant walls, called a portaledge. Each morning for a couple weeks, I woke up suspended from the ceiling for a second thinking, "where am I?" looking out their windows to the sunshine and snow covered mountains of Crested Butte.

Collective couch surfing is another term I recently heard of from local Greg Pettys, who helped me research this article. Let's use the famous Cebolla Lodge in Gunnison, located next to another landmark, The Ski Fence House, for example. There you have what is known as a climbers' house. It has been kept in the climbing family for a couple years with one climber living there for a few months, then another moving in. One winter, the climbers got so bored they bolted chains to the ceiling, so they could practice dangling from them with ice axes for strength training. The landlord was not happy about this one.

Next to the climbers' place, live two hip girls who have all sorts of interesting companions. At any time in the spring, summer, or fall (winter can be a rough season), there are up to six surfers, rarely working, using their friend's place as a base camp for adventures in the outdoors. One surfer is a mountain guide who just returned from a season on Mt. Shasta in California. He sleeps in his truck with every possession he owns. Another, who works in wilderness therapy in Utah, is next to him in the parking lot in her van. A professional outdoorsman, who works with troubled youth half the year and travels around the world the other half, sleeps inside on the futon. A mountain biker, who is also a graduate student, stays on the couch and up to three raft guides can be found passed out on the floor, or on the front deck.

This way of life, somehow titled couch surfing, reflects the interesting mountain culture in the Gunnison Valley. It shows how generous people are, provided one embraces the concept of karma, what goes around comes around. People homeless by choice, sacrificing having a home to call their own, are usually in the pursuit of a dream. That dream may be simply to climb a mountain, or just to get more skiing days in this season. It may be to save enough money to spend the entire winter kayaking in Costa Rica, climbing in Joshua Tree, or volunteering in Africa.

Whatever the cause, the couch surfing network will take in the adventurers, with too much soul to be labeled freeloaders, people living a modern version of the American Dream. Of course they will only be welcome if they understand the customs, the way of the couch surfer. They accept the world is their home, riding a wave of opportunity and creativity, with perfect timing.

A version of this story was originally published in the Crested Butte Magazine, Winter 2007-2008.

6 WEIRD AND WHEELED ENCOUNTERS IN HITCHHIKER'S SPACE

Damn, will this be the night no one picks me up? The stars are coming out and I've been waiting for over a half an hour. "Be patient," I tell myself. "Someone always stops."

Finally, after a forty five minute wait, a car slows down and the driver rolls down the window, "Are you going to Gunnison?" I ask.

"Sure am," the young driver answers.

"Sweet," my doubts dissolved and I settle in for the ride. So what's this guy all about, I wonder. I soon find out. He's just finished his first year at Western State, and has decided to stick around for the summer. He's excited about everything. Oh, to be new to the Gunnison Valley, Colorado, and to experience the pleasures of the summer for the first time!

"So, do you go to Western State?" he asks me.

I think it's my baby face that leads most people to assume that. "No, I graduated a couple years ago."

"What do you do?" he asks.

"Well, I'm a dishwasher, but I really want to be a writer," I explain.

We go through the standard hitchhiking dialogue till the point in the conversation where we're interested in what each other is saying or we're just talking to talk. I know the routine by now, as I've picked up a hundred hitchhikers and hitchhiked more than a hundred times.

It's a system that works well in the Gunnison Valley. No car, gas prices too expensive to drive to work, or just in need of a quick adventure to the opposite end of the valley? Just head out towards the highway and stick out your thumb. Eventually, someone will stop.

Sometimes you'll be picked up in thirty seconds, other times one can wait an hour. When times are rough and no one is stopping, rather than getting angry, I try to remind myself of the previous positive experiences I've had. And sometimes, not always, just the right person will stop, and at just the right moment.

One morning, late as hell for work, after waiting an hour for a ride, a large SUV stopped to pick me up. Those big gas guzzlers are the ones that don't usually stop, but after confirming that the driver was headed to Crested Butte, I happily jumped in the truck. After a few minutes of relative silence, we started to talk with the usual, "So what do you do?"

He was delighted to find out that I was a writer and revealed to me that he was a retired stunt man and currently writes scripts for movies. "See that hill up there," he says. "I worked on a film with John Wayne on that hillside. That's how I discovered the Gunnison Valley. Now my wife and I live here in the summers. We live in Los Angeles during the winter."

"So what do you write about?" he asks me.

"Mostly about my rock climbing adventures," I answered. "I'm writing a book right now."

"Oh yeah, that's great. I worked with Sylvester Stallone on Cliffhanger. Have you heard of that?"

"Of course," I answered. "Those climbing scenes were pretty unrealistic, though."

"I know. We told the director, but he wouldn't listen." He went on explaining the details and politics of making a Hollywood movie. "You know, you should register your book once you're done with it, so that no one steals your work. The real money would be in turning your book into a movie."

We slowly roll into CB and he keeps going with the advice, "It's a hard thing to be a writer. It takes a lot of personal discipline. Just keep it up okay?"

"Yes sir, I sure will."

It's impressive the wealth of interesting people that are attracted to the Gunnison Valley. Another older man, a mountaineer, has picked me up a couple times.

"Yeah, I think I still have the record for number of trips up Denali," he said.

"Wow," I sincerely reply.

"I'm coming back from Denver from physical therapy," he tells me. "I broke my neck up on K2. We were close to the top when it happened, and we had a choice; we could go down, or we could keep going. We kept going."

Hitchhikers get to hear the best stories, and you never know who will tell them. This May, a Crested Butte Mountain Resort employee, dressed like your average Joe from the city, collared shirt, short hair, driving a Hyundai, picked me up. I was sure the ride was going to be a bore. Ten minutes into the ride, he was telling me about the time he hitchhiked from Denver to Central America. "I was eighteen, and a friend and I decided to see how far we could get on a few hundred dollars. He ran out of money in Panama, but I made it all the way to Columbia."

Later, he was telling me of his second big hitching adventure. "Then, I went to Europe and hitched all the way to Iran. I ended up in an opium den, with the chief of police and his friends," he said with a reflective look. "They wanted me to stay and marry one of their daughters."

We rolled into Gunnison, and I was sad for the ride to end, "Thanks for letting me tell these stories. My kids have heard them all."

Not all rides have great chemistry, though. Hitchhiking can provoke awkwardness, out of place propositions, fear and sometimes danger. In this past summer alone, I've experienced a man I'd only known for a few minutes who wanted to sell me LSD, a guy who wanted to convert me over to Christianity, and a fellow who drove 85 miles an hour the whole way to Gunnison, even through the Almont curves. The worst possible hitchhiking scenario was told to me by the local coroner, who, despite his occupation, is a friendly, light human being.

"Hitchhiking certainly comes with risk," he said. "A few years ago, at this corner up here, just before Almont, there was a car accident, and the hitchhiker was the only one who died."

I quickly changed the subject, and we started discussing other things. We talked of the recent boom in Crested Butte, of poetry and ranching. This ride provided storytelling, instant friendship and education, all in thirty minutes.

"You're family has been in The Valley a long time huh?" I asked him.

"Yeah, most of the family history is tied with ranching," he responded.

"The Valley sure is changing," I offered. "There's more and more development."

"There is, but I think ranching and real estate development can coexist, if the developers just don't mess with the valleys that are ideal for grazing" he said.

"I have a lot of respect for ranchers," I responded. "Everyone benefits from their work with these open views," I added as I looked across the green fields off the highway.

"Boy I sure could have made a lot of money in real estate if I would've had a few thousand dollars in the seventies," he said, a sentiment I've heard from many mid-timers.

Another common conversation piece I've heard from the mid-timers of the Gunnison Valley is the wild partying scene of CB in the seventies. "Man, even the cops were into it," a guy told me on the way to Crested Butte one day. "You work at Donita's Cantina? Man that place used to be wild."

"Oh yeah?"

The partying stories of the old glory days used to interest me, but they're all pretty much the same. "I quit drinking, though," he added, but went on with the same old stories till we got close to Crested Butte.

"Could you drop me off in Skyland?" I asked.

"Sure, that's actually where I'm going too," he said. "Hey, how would you like to make twenty bucks?"

"Doing what?"

"Unloading this carpet in the back of the truck," he says. An hour later, I'd just finished my first construction work in the Valley. "If you're interested in some more work, just give me a call," my employer for the hour said.

"Well, I'm not now, but maybe in the off season."

Everything changes in the off season, and I suppose that's the hardest season for hitchhiking. Off seasons always end though, and soon enough its winter. Winters seem to have the most hitchhiking traffic, many of whom are Mexicans that come to work for the ski resort.

I rarely pass a hitchhiker by, and I especially never pass a Mexican by for one reason, a free Spanish lesson. What a system: opportunities to work on your second language, meeting people you might never get to otherwise, and reducing your consumption of gasoline, while saving money; the possibilities of hitchhiking are endless.

My personal best, most important ride started off differently than most. It was a girl. She was around my age, and she was cute. I soon found out she had just moved to the Gunnison Valley from Boulder, and was psyched to be out of the city and into small mountain town living. The ride ended as most do, with a "thanks for the ride," and a quick exit at a stop sign.

A winter went by, and a spring and a summer, too. The next fall, after my first international hitchhiking experience in Central America, I saw the cute girl again on campus at Western State. She had a beautiful tan from a summer of raft guiding, and despite the butterflies in my stomach, I just had to talk to her. Talking led to a climbing date, and that led to a few months of dating. The love changed with the seasons, as it many times does, but it was love all the same. And it may never have happened if I hadn't decided to hitchhike that day.

I rarely hitchhike anymore, and in most areas of our country couldn't even imagine doing so. The Gunnison Valley area is unique in many ways, and probably one of the safest places to hitch a ride in the United States. Writing that hitchhiking is safe, though, would be like saying rock climbing is safe; there is always a risk. On this angle of repose, it's hard to regret using this system of transportation. Remembering that I stuck my thumb out, relying on the kindness of a stranger with a seat open in their vehicle to share.

A version of this story was originally published in the Crested Butte Magazine, Winter 2006-2007.

7 THIS IS BUILDERING

In the deep of the twilight, the night, buzzed on something, spirits, smoke, the usual, a change occurs: an athletic alchemy, different urges, some of the chances and opportunities of the night have passed, with no possibility of getting laid, you've stayed up too late to get really good sleep, some sense to experience more, and not just sit around and talk about things, besides the bartender is telling you to leave, stumbling out onto the streets, some think, 'one more cigarette or a bong session, perhaps a silly movie, maybe the twelve pack of Pabst Blue Ribbon in the fridge at home?'

Others think about climbing buildings.

Enter the mind and body of a climber, in an urban concrete jungle we call a city. Enter their heart thumping and pumping blood. Look through their eyes at the buildings with a desire that no one but a climber could feel, an inclination to interact with them, to enter a different dimension, the vertical realm, one with substantial risk. The usual risks of climbing: the consequences from falling, abuse to joints, bones and muscles. Also, legal risks: trespassing, the chance a cop may drive by and see you, though he would hardly think to look for someone twenty feet up the side of a building at three in the morning.

When most everyone has entered the dreamworld of sleep, or other lazy activities in the horizontal, the lucky ones are, well, getting lucky. In a town of thousands, just two or three may decide to enter the vertical. They will choose to builder.

For a few years now, I've managed to stay primarily on the outside of buildering sessions, while still remaining on the inside. While I've gotten off the ground a time or two, usually I just watch, especially when the building at hand enters the zone, when a fall could mean death. Just being around the excitement is enough for me, and in the last few years, for many nights after the bars close, I've found myself within a cipher of builderers trying to climb anything they please, mixing their beer buzz with adrenaline, putting their youthful health on the line for an intense rush.

I don't know if Sparks builders much these days, but he did, and during a winter night in a cold town called Gunnison, Colorado, he had one of those mystical, magical moments, which involved several elements, as you'll see.

Sparks is one of those climbers, that people must think of when they visualize a guy in his twenties, who muscles his way through a rock climb. Ripped, like the guys posing on the packages of underwear. For some reason, his climbing performance rarely matched up with his strength. Climbing requires a mental discipline, a vertical meditation that often Sparks lacked. When his mind was on an off day, he could not perform on the rock, he could not complete the difficult move because his mind would not focus. Though his body was strong enough, often his mind would not break through to the meditative state needed for difficult climbing. But he was strong, way strong, and once in a full moon, he would be on and great things could happen.

Well it may have been a full moon, the coyotes must've been howlin', cause that night, amidst the psychedelics and the beer, we were climbing everything that looked like it could be climbed: the outside of a ten-foot stucco ATM station next to the bank, with an overhanging bulge near the finish and a foot of snow on the top, a plastic horse that was a sign for a local cowboy shop which was twelve feet off the ground, also covered in snow, even a route that was so difficult it hasn't seen a known repeat ascent in years on Main Street, a route climbing up the front side of the sketchiest bar in town.

It was one of those nights when people were in town for the holidays. The snow was falling like it's supposed to in the mountains, maybe an inch an hour accumulating on rooftops, streets and sidewalks. Spirits were flowing. Christmas lights were lit, like we all were, buzzed so much that at a point in the party no one could come up with a reason why we shouldn't go out. This was one of those nights. We were a group of climbers, and a couple girls that liked climber dudes, who were along for the kicks.

Climbers, especially the ones that are in their young twenties, are scruffy and rough around the edges, many have unkept beards, pants and clothes with holes in them; a result of spending money first on gear and road tripping and second on clothing. No surprise, they also tend to be open minded. Climbing rocks, mountains, and in this case, buildings, requires a free mind that can come up with creative solutions to challenges. In addition to this, climbers must create a sense of believing, a sort of willing the body through dangerous and improbable situations. This is a positive characteristic that successful climbers share, and it is no surprise many people say climbing works at creating metaphors for life.

Give climbers a little booze and this open mindedness can get them into trouble. Like this night, where minds were altered by some additional things, and we were climbing all over town as if the structures in town were just rocks, eyeing a building that looked climbable and giving it a go, ignoring whether it was affiliated with a bank, a church or the government. Add some success on a couple of routes, which provided some sweet adrenaline and there was quite a cocktail of chemicals running through the veins.

So after Sparks had climbed the ATM machine, had a few drinks at the bar, and walked a mile across town in six inches of snow, he was ready for anything. A free mind, egged on by six intoxicated spirits, high and completely stoned into the winter moment. That *anything* Sparks was ready for led us to the entrance of the sketchiest bar in town, the Alamo, a place known for coke usage in the bathroom and a constant haze of cigarette smoke hanging over the pool tables and the patrons. Outside was a large, thirty foot vertical sign that read P I Z Z A, which probably confused some tourists each year to walk into the place and find no pizza, just second hand smoke, beer and a handful of souls there to escape whatever it was that led them to the 'Mo. Leading up to the infamous, out of place pizza sign is a difficult buildering route, which as we walked by, caught the attention of our group.

The start of the building is what appears to be some average masonry, big stones a foot tall and two feet wide cemented into the wall, protruding out a couple inches so that they make great climbing holds, not at all symmetric, but, hey, we're talking about a shady bar here. These perfect holds lead up to a wooden, shingled roof, slightly angled and, this night, covered in ten inches of snow. Just a foot right of the route was the entrance to the bar.

Now two or three of us had made it to this point before Sparks and found the move too precarious and difficult to attempt. The move wasn't very dangerous, only eight feet off the ground, so a fall was relatively safe, especially with five spotters below, with their hands up, ready to protect the climber from hurting himself.

Sparks was on fire, and you could see it in his eyes and feel it in the energy that surrounded him. After an unsuccessful attempt, he was about to climb back onto the bar when a bouncer poked his head out, eyes glazed over from a night of complimentary shift drinks. He looked at Sparks with one of those, "what the hell are you doing?" looks. Sparks quickly acted like he was just checking out the well-done masonry work and glanced back at us, rubbing the wall, "Yeah, this is real nice isn't it?"

The drunken bouncer went back inside confused. Sparks immediately got back on the wall and in thirty seconds reached the nearly horizontal roof. This move was the crux, the most difficult buildering sequence that had been attempted all night. In a sober state, it would be very hard, and Sparks' mind might have not been able to break through and conceive the move, but fueled with the adrenaline cocktail, he didn't think, he just acted. Like a karate master, he swung his foot above his head off to his right and planted it into the snow on the roof. As he dug his foot into the snow a couple, arm in arm, stumbled out of the bar, their expression quickly turned from intoxicated lust to amazement and terror as they looked up to see Sparks rocking his foot onto the snow covered roof, pushing his hands down and moving onto the roof.

He'd conquered the Alamo.

As the snow continued to fall and the couple walked away uttering drunken babble, Sparks climbed down a ladder on the backside of the bar to receive his prize, hugs and high-fives from his crowd of admirers.

Conditions in the winter were far from ideal for buildering in Gunnison; ice and snow made climbs more difficult and cold temperatures made it harder to grip holds with numb fingertips. But it made sense during the winter. Climbers don't get that rush that they are dependent upon as often, the rush that comes from getting scared and using the muscles of one's body to the utmost extent.

I knew I was dependent on that fix as much as the guys in the Alamo were dependent on their numerous shots of Jack Daniels and the nicotine from Marlboro Reds. Hell, I'd been addicted to numerous things before I started climbing and I knew I was hooked on the climbing buzz.

That may have been some self therapy there, because it doesn't exactly provide the segue I was looking for, but it brings us to the next part of the story, the summertime, where a climber in Gunnison could get that fix any time he or she wanted to, provided they didn't have to work and it wasn't raining. Gunnison is surrounded by rocks (they don't call 'em the Rocky Mountains for nuthin') in every direction and someone was always psyched to go climbing.

But there were still some of the usual reasons to builder, not getting any lovin', and, well, you were fired up from partying all night, and there was no reason to go home.

This summertime buildering session occurred during the typical hours, just after the bar closed at two thirty in the morning. The group consisted of yours truly, P-Real, B-Boy Roy, T-Drizzle and Lucy. The stars shined bright, the moon lit the town up as much as the streetlights. The air was cool as it always is in a mountain town at night. The streetlights lit up one side of an old church, which was the first climbing objective for the evening. I was pleased that the first building was something that had to do with religion and not the law, thinking that trespassing with the church would provide less harsh consequences than the government. From what I'd heard, nothing was off limits that particular summer: banks, government buildings, rumor had it one night these guys even climbed on the police station. So we arrived at the church, a forty foot tall, white brick building, which appeared to be from the early nineteen hundreds, that narrowed as it went higher, slender at the top, with a four foot tall cross on the tiny roof.

The first attempted climb was too hard, and it was dark, as neither the moon nor the streetlights illuminated it. The moves were big reaches for small holds, on the white bricks that a fingertip pad would barely fit on. No one got too far, and I was glad because the climb would have finished forty feet off the ground and a fall from up there would involve some other people in uniforms we would rather not have contact with, Emergency Medical Technicians.

So we moved around the church following P-Real, who was the reason behind the partying that evening, considering it was his birthday. P-Real found a route that was to his liking, with bigger bricks to hold onto, a path of least resistance to the top of the church.

Examining the psyche of P-Real would reveal that he has his

mind mastered to a higher level than our friend Sparks. Unlike Sparks, P-Real has a mind that is just as tuned for climbing as his body. Watching P-Real climb was like watching a master of the rock, not necessarily all the time, for this was just the 23rd birthday, not enough experience to become perfect in the vertical terrain, but he'd shown that he had what it took to be a successful climber. He's also a southern boy, which in Gunnison made him stand apart from nearly every other climber. P-Real was a remarkable and unique character, that everyone in the climbing community knew, or knew of. So all four of us listened, when in his distinct southern drawl he looked up at the arête on the side of the church and uttered slowly in a rather monotone way, "I'm gonna climb this fucker."

So off he went up the church, which conveniently was facing both the moon and the streetlights. P-Real climbed in his trademark warrior way, no hesitation, no hint of nervousness, fluid movement from brick to brick, which protruded from the side of the church generously and at equal increments. In this manner, he quickly entered a zone, thirty feet off the ground where a fall would be disastrous. Though he had four of us spotting him, we could do little to protect him from a six step concrete stairway that lay directly in his fall path. A metal railing eight feet long to the left of the stairs ensured that if P-Real fell, things would be bad, real bad. The stairway and railing was an emergency exit for church patrons, but for P-Real, if he were to fall down on this, it would spell disaster, and possibly a chance to meet his maker.

All of us spotters, T-Drizzle, Lucy, B-Boy Roy and yours truly, gave each other a look. A look that we didn't need to put into words that P-Real could hear. The look that had the intensity that a normal serious climbing situation would have, but this was different: it was three in the morning, and this southern boy thirty feet above us on the side of a church had been drinking whiskey all night.

"You got this P-Real," Roy said, defying what he may have been thinking, but sending up necessary encouragement.

"Yeah, man, looking good," T-Drizzle added.

P-Real climbed five feet higher and was near the lip of the roof of the church, just below the cross, into the unknown. He had no idea what it would be like, and since none of us had climbed it, we couldn't offer any beta. As he reached up to the top of the church, a small chunk of brick falls down to the ground, hitting the rail, and making a "clink" sound. Unfazed and buzzed on adrenaline, P-Real kept searching for a handhold, the sound of his breathing just slightly increased.

A minute later, he was still in the same spot, his left hand is feeling to top of the church for a hold. Another small chunk of brick, quarter sized, fell down, this time landing on the grass. This prompted Lucy to speak her first words since P-Real left the ground, with a tone of a mother that has warned her disobeying children one time too many, "P-Real you get down from there right now!"

A cold silence followed her words, and immediately P-Real started his retreat, gently climbing down the bricks, forty feet back to the ground, back to the horizontal. Lucy gave him a motherly look, we all offered a handshake, and with that P-Real had survived another birthday, and another buildering session had ended.

T-Drizzle, B-Boy Roy and P-Real made it through the summer without suffering any injuries. However, the more I talked about buildering with friends the more I heard stories where people got hurt doing it. Ironically, these people were usually top notch climbers, who had spent countless days taking big risks on big walls and boulders, and these were their most severe injuries.

Regardless, just as STDs don't stop random drunken hookups, people will still continue to builder. There is a fire lit in the spirit of youth, an energy some express by doing graffiti on billboards and trains, which some call art and others vandalism. Others may skateboard, putting their energy into that sport, onto the concrete, grinding a rail in a park. Some see skateboarding as trouble, others use it to keep out of trouble.

Buildering is very risky, but it is also an expression: a manifestation of energies, in the twilight, buzzed, not ready for the night to end, determined to live more, to transform. To builder.

8 A CLIMBER IN THE WINTER OF HIS DISCONTENT

He has always given climbing the utmost of his attention and energy, but I know he would rather fall in love. However, falling in love isn't easy, and going to climb some rocks is.

He has climbed throughout the west, coming of age and learning some truths about his life, that it will most certainly end, but it has the possibility to find happiness that most don't get to feel.

He knew the feeling of love was more powerful and lasting than the feeling of scraping up a big chunk of granite or bouldering in a desert paradise. Well, he thought he knew this, but he really only hoped. From all the lonely, old climbers he had met, he knew there was no way he wanted to end up like them. They were probably just as happy as he was at twenty five, and assumed all they needed was themselves. High on marijuana, and conquering rocks they definitely one day thought might be impossible, high on the feeling of indestructibility, that is just as false as the drunk's feeling that he can drive home after a night at the bar.

He hoped he wouldn't end up like them, but maybe he wouldn't even live to see his forties. If there was one thing he'd learned from failing in love and succeeding on climbs, it was to appreciate the moment.

It's hard to appreciate the moment when the rocks will be covered with snow for four more months, and the only warm climbing outlet is the greasy holds at the college gym, when you live in a place that calls itself the Coldest City of the Lower 48, and you've pursued every decent looking woman you know to see if there is a spark of interest.

He knows love will come his way someday, so he lives with hope. Quitting his daily pot habit only made him more in tune with his desperate situation, but he accepted it all the same. In that cold time, he would rather fall in love than have the opportunity to climb any particular rock. He'd trade a couple days in the vertical for a good opportunity in the horizontal. He walks around town, hanging in the coffee shops and bars, pretending he's not looking for love, but the thought dominates in his mind.

I'm sure, well I hope, love will find him when he least expects it, at the time when he should expect it. Grasping the same climbing holds in the local area he fell in love with long ago, he might look over and see a beautiful woman. In the climbing competitions at the college, she may be there. Will she be impressed with his skills he developed by focusing more on climbing than academics during his college years? She may be in the computer lab he is writing this from right now.

Like a big climb, it's impossible to know what might happen next; it's best to stay in the present. It's best to stay in the present even if it's fifteen below zero, you're down to your last dollar and you won't be paid for another three days.

He's lived in Gunnison for enough time to appreciate the suffering, knowing that is the path of the mountain writer, of the climber. At the same time, he dreams of those perfect days climbing a sexy wall when he is the most alive; the days that are logged in to the back of his memory, for cold alone days like this one.

He has learned to respect the cold, knowing it's the only way to know the warm; the only way to know a good day is to have a bad one. The coldest city in Colorado provides the perfect environment for a person like him, life on the edge, where he can survive on a few grand a year and be satisfied.

He has found you don't have to ski to be a modern mountain man. You don't have to make a lot of money to be rich. And when one is so far away from love, that's the time you want it the most.

9 SOMEWHERE BETWEEN DREAMS AND SMOG IS LOVE

This basement I'm living in is cold. It's surrounded by slowly deteriorating concrete walls, with kids' chalk writing from previous tenants. There's a pool table that never gets used, and a heater that makes a lot of noise, forcing all the heat upstairs. It's chilly down here, not cold enough to see your breath cold, but close. I always sleep in too late. The basement is dark, and it is a struggle to decide what is better, oversleeping or venturing out into cold and smoggy, Salt Lake City, Utah. Sleep usually wins.

I envy the hibernating bear.

My dreams are usual dreams, I think. How could I really know what your dreams are like? I sleep too much, so maybe I dream too much as well. Lately, and by lately I mean the last three years since I graduated from college, I've been living this thing called the climbing dream. One just lives on very little money, camps out in a tent, surfs a couch or two, and climbs rocks as much as possible. It's pretty sweet, and the last few years have taken me from Colorado to Utah, California, Oregon and Mexico.

Now, I have tendonitis and the climbing dream, well, I've had to wake up from that. While I recover, the new dream is exploring my mind through writing, as much as possible. Recently, I had an editor tell me I write about being a writer too much. I guess my life is at that stage where I'm trying to transform a dream to reality. And sometimes you have to constantly remind yourself of the goal and the dream.

My dreams come from wherever they come from. I sleep on a blue shag carpet, covering up the concrete floor, in an old sleeping bag my friend found on the side of the highway. Years of camping have made beds feel uncomfortable. I only sleep in beds when I'm with a woman, though I like it best to make love outdoors. So I wake up late, like one o'clock in the afternoon late, my own personal form of hibernation.

The bike ride on the way through the city on my townie, I hop on, sometimes wishing I had the entire protective armor, the helmet and the facemask. I breathe and inevitably inhale smog. They say living in the pollution here is like smoking five cigarettes a day. I pay more attention to the immediate risk, the motorists, and the threat of getting hit by a car. I always count down the blocks.

I am close, as the little blinking electronic white man says I can cross the intersection. For a second I feel free, as if the person in the Hummer I just barely made eye contact with is a prisoner to her vehicle. Seconds later, I am the prisoner as I wait, the fleet of vehicles pass by, from the bling new white Mercedes with shiny rims, to the rusted red and blue Ford truck from the sixties; the daily parade of Salt Lake City.

My destination is the library, downtown baby. It is a beacon of light, a symbol of freedom and knowledge, a safe haven in the city. I walk by a bum, I see him everyday, he just stares straight ahead. What is he thinking about? I hear the *click, click, clicking* of high heels coming from behind me, a young professional woman. I smell coffee from the little shop inside. People stare into laptops for hours; some have those earpiece cell phones. When these people talk on those types of phones, they look similar to the crazy homeless guys who talk to themselves while walking down the street.

I check my email. I am a slave to the computer; rarely do I go a day without using it. When I leave the computer and sit down at a desk, I find freedom in writing. My own space, all to myself, I love the library, and I love our country for this place.

On the second floor of this four story building, I look out the glass windows to the city. White mountains provide a backdrop to the buildings of the city. A haze of smog lies in between, while below people go back and forth. A train takes some away, and leaves others off as they scatter to do their work and follow their own dreams.

When I put the pen to the paper, the words usually write themselves, or nothing happens. Sometimes the words slowly come with some extra patience, like convincing a lover to spend some more time. I believe the words want to come onto the page. Today the words flow like the river does into the ocean, from the pen on to the paper. Sometimes I just stop and bask in the meditation.

My dream is to become a famous writer, but I think just being alive and in this zone of freedom is the greatest reward. I also ponder does not the famous writer always have to face the blank page again?

If I was still dreaming, and I knew it, what would I do?

Would I ask the homeless man to go out to lunch with me? Would that help him with his troubles? Would it help me with mine? Would I tell the alluring woman, with her face as fresh as flowers, as she checks out my books, that she is beautiful? In the most sincere way, directly from my heart chakra, bypassing the ego? Is she thinking similar thoughts about me? Are there all kinds of thoughts and emotions we don't say that just get buried away? I think there are because when I start to open up, I don't want to stop.

I live to love and long for women. When I am confident and have a glide in my stride, they seem right there, approachable, like all I would do is suggest getting together sometime, and then we could be wrapped up in each other's prose over lettuce wraps and cloves, and later, if the feeling was right, without clothes? Intertwined.

I rarely get the conversation flow going with girls that aren't in a circle, of work, climbing, friends of friends, so I just look at her with that shyness defense mechanism illuminating from my facial features, and in that ever fleeting moment the book about romance and love is checked out, and there I go.

In the supermarket there was this girl, who I saw one day, a less confident day, the kind of day where you're just going through the motions, like a machine, probably slept in too late in that basement.

The sexy woman whose curly, red hair went long past her breasts, and her bangs went so close to her eyes that she became something of a mystery as I waited to check out. Her illumination appeared to be sexually genius, a secure female swagger, a vibe in her stride, like she was sacred and just a few men had ever entered her temple, as she asked, "paper or plastic?"

I had my own bag but nothing clever to say, or even to ask how she was doing. This was not an on day. The girl, though, right in front of me seemed a thousand miles away, like a new Mercedes in the car lot to a guy who makes minimum wage. It's sad, when the possibility of physical love seems so far from becoming reality, for I love women. I dream to taste their mouths and be together for hours, to share my masculinity in trade for femininity, to bask in a dreamlike yin and yang of raw, healthy, human sexuality.

"No bag, I've got one," are the only words I say here while my mind is off in space. I get back on my bike, and think even the worst days give me something to write about. Dreaming is great, but it always leads to the same place, either more dreams or waking up to this world. So my salvation must live in the actions of the tangible world, real some call it, because I won't find love in dreams. I'll only find it as my conscious self, and in the infinite beauty and countless beauties that surround me.

10 THE UNDERWEAR MODEL STORY

My dream job would be modeling underwear. A friend helped me figure this out one day after I'd just purchased some new undies, and we were looking at the models on the packaging.

"What a job that would be, wearing underwear for a living," I said.

"You could do it," Amber answered. "And since you're a climber you could model for Patagonia."

A quick check of the Patagonia catalog showed that they didn't use the same advertising technique that we imagined; my visual image was Victoria Secret style for the female models. Still the dream was planted.

Winter, Salt Lake City, Utah, I'm on a date with a girl I met at the local raw food restaurant. Her house: throwback, psychedelic, complete with record player, Polaroid camera, and a little fireplace we sat next to and talked. She's the intuitive type, the kind of girl who references her dreams often, and talks of love and living in harmony with the planet.

In her room later, she's showing me energy stones and waxing poetic. For some reason, I mention that I'm going to the Patagonia outlet store in the morning for a sale. Then she begins to tell me about a dream she had. The focus of the dream: me just wearing a fire red pair of underwear. We kiss and then she sends me out into the cold night.

The next morning, my friend Sara and I are up at the crack of dawn, waiting behind a hundred or so shoppers as the line pours out, winding around the store. Sara is a good friend, one I consider a sister, and to top that off she's letting me couch surf at her house for the month.

Later, waiting in line to check out, we're behind a hundred and fifty or so people, and there's a box of underwear. I tell Sara about the ladyfriend's dream. She looks in and sees a fire red pair, tosses it into my bag and says, "Maybe you'll get lucky."

The following night, I'm taking off my clothes. Clear sky, the stars above and mountains blanketed in snow. Sara and I are at the Midway hot springs. The scene is strange; Lynyrd Skynyrd blasts out of a trailer-truck. A fellow, who appears to be on some sort of crack, is doing flips in the hundred and ten degree water. A fog emits from the springs, and I can't identify my surroundings other than the Skynyrd and the people in the springs. It feels like the beginning of a horror movie.

The idea of kicking back in the hot springs doesn't seem relaxing anymore. Still there are hot springs to be soaked in. I strip down, almost all the way down to what else, my new red underwear. Was this the scene that my ladyfriend imagined? With the cover of my new underwear, I slipped into the heat and the weirdness of the hot springs.

I never got to hang out with the young psychedelic woman again, but I think of her every time I wear my red underwear. I know I would feel comfortable in them in many different situations, and after the odd hot springs experience, being in front of a camera would be pretty chill. So Patagonia, if you have an opening for some underwear models, give me a call.

This piece was originally published on Patagonia's blog, The Cleanest Line.

11 WILD MOUNTAIN HONEY

'It's a shame the single mountain women are complained about more than celebrated, for they are more beautiful than the mountains themselves,' he thought, as two young women passed him as he hiked along Tony's Trail.

All the cliché sayings he's heard about mountain women. "You don't lose your girlfriend, you just lose your turn," and of course the ever uttered, "There's no women in this town." A phrase he often heard from a fool's mouth, while he sat on a barstool and a woman stood right behind him.

Though his heart had been broken several times, he still had the utmost respect for the mountain women. A wise friend once told him you can only truly live or love after your heart has been crushed. The hope of meeting another Mountain Honey filled him with desire and longing, as strong as a shivering person camping in the cold, waiting for the sun to rise.

He took another step along the trail, then he looked back to admire the women, as they rode by on their mountain bikes. They had the look: strong legs, shining faces, and beautiful hair that bounced down to their breasts. He recognized the two, married perhaps, definitely not available. Some say all the good ones are taken, but had these beauties not once arrived to The Valley single? They probably arrived in beat up old pickup trucks, perhaps intending only to stay for a summer in the mountains, full of energy and life, wild as the wind, full of so much love that had to be met with the love of someone else.

He thought of what he wanted, what he needed, and what he had experienced before. There were the nights making love under the autumn stars, the wildest and purest emotions erupting into the most fabulous sensations he'd ever known. Then to wake up naked, freezing in the middle of the night, as he and his lover climbed into the pickup truck for shelter.

Then there were the endless winters without love, when he had no confidence to approach women. Followed by the birth of spring, and the rebirth of self, and knowing his confidence would be restored, he could and would again manifest love. That just as the birds always sing again, and the flowers will bloom, he would love again.

He took another step on the trail. It was June, but spring was still in the air. The flowers had yet to bloom in Crested Butte, but the sagebrush smelled as sweet as ever. With the current of possibilities of how amazing the summer could be, he looked down to the town of Crested Butte. A Mountain Honey, surely there was one for him down there. He had confidence in his steps, as town grew closer. He knew as summer grew closer, he was closer to the most fabulous joy on earth, romancing with a Wild Mountain Honey.

12 HAMMER'S TIME

When you're young and filled with energy, Halloween is the greatest of opportunities to act out some fantasies, and live close to that line that separates fact from fiction.

Now I don't know if that explains why Styles was dressed up as a blow up doll, complete with fake boobs, a tight fitting plastic body suit and a face full of makeup, but it certainly explains why Rick dressed up as the nineties dancing machine, hip-hop artist that called himself MC Hammer.

The day started with rummaging through costumes at the local thrift store on the day of Halloween. Procrastination is something college students seem to excel at, and the Boomerang in Gunnison, Colorado, was packed with people trying to find a last minute get up. Styles and Rick wanted to be the center of attention, and to entertain the people. Most of all they hoped to make people laugh.

Rick picked out a pair of baggy, shiny, purple pants, a black vest, a gold chain and a flat top wig. Styles, who prepares for Halloween with more enthusiasm than nearly everyone else, had purchased his costume three weeks previously on E-Bay, and was already in costume attracting points and smiles from the shoppers in the store.

Back at Rick's apartment, he was pondering his costume. Could he really pull off MC Hammer, one of the most memorable characters from the nineties? Would his costume be convincing? Would this be a classic Halloween or a bust?

"They're going to think you're Vanilla Ice," Styles joked.

Rick hoped that wouldn't happen, and tried to visualize what Hammer looked like when he saw him in real life, randomly shopping in the Mall of America in Minnesota. That must have been the moment that made Hammer a hero to him. Rick and his friend were the first ones to notice him shopping. When he left the store, sixty people were following him around, as if he were some sort of prophet.

Rick focused on that image, put on an old Hammer tape and practiced his dance moves. The "Hammer Dance" was unique and recognizable. A series of sideways shuffles, a turnaround spin, jump back and forth, all while making his baggy pants float in the air!

"Damn, you've actually got some skills," Blow Up Doll said, surprised.

Now if you could imagine, a male blow up doll, highlighted with blue and red makeup in a bright neon green body suit, and high heels, walking in a stiff manner next to a white MC Hammer, complete with the extra baggy pants that fluffed in the wind, a boom box, a gold chain, walking as if he owned the nineties, and, for that matter, as if he owned the street they were crossing in broad daylight to get a cup of coffee.

Hammer felt liberated, as if he was getting ready for the show of his life. Blow Up Doll felt awkward, already complaining about the stiffness of his outfit. The next stop after coffee was the LQ, the liquor store, where Blow Up Doll could get some liquid confidence for the evening. Hammer had agreed to be the designated driver, a real DD. In previous years, the DD simply didn't drink but was allowed to dabble in hallucinogenics, which the duo agreed, if they kept up this practice, the whole Halloween crew might be eliminated from the gene pool.

As nighttime approached they cruised over to Rex's house. Rex was dressed up as a skiing cowboy from Texas; we'll call him the Million Dollar Cowboy. He wore a cowboy hat, a jean jacket, blue jeans and ski boots. He walked awkwardly around the house practicing his accent saying things like, "Yee-haw! If this ain't goin to be a darn tootin' get up good ol' hell of a time tonight."

The Dude from The Big Lebowski was also there, as well as Ed Viesturs, the legendary mountaineer. The Million Dollar Cowboy kept rubbing on Blow Up Doll's boobs and Hammer was getting defensive, "That ain't legit Cowboy, get your hands off her, ummm, I mean him."

Everyone was beginning to act in character, and thus the true spirit of Halloween was coming through. The Dude was sipping white Russians and trying to keep everyone calm, "I've got to meet my lady friend now, man, so everyone stay cool," he said in a hippie, stoned like slow voice.

The Mountaineer sat at the farthest end of the kitchen table, and no one noticed how fast he was drinking cans of Pabst Blue Ribbon. "We need more beer," he proclaimed.

As the Dude made an exit to his lady friend's house, wearing only a bathrobe to protect him from the cold Colorado night, the quirky quintet decided to get out and find parties. Since Hammer was the DD, he took the wheel of the party-mobile for the night, an old Toyota RV, called the Dolphin.

The Dolphin had a hundred stories of its own. It had been to Alaska and back, to Vegas on Phish tour, it had seen many road trips and a few LSD trips as well. The crew got comfortable in the Dolphin as the Million Dollar Cowboy said, "Gawd dang, let's get this party started."

The plan was to go to a college party in Gunnison, then cruise up the highway thirty miles to Crested Butte. With six years of college experience under his belt, Hammer predicted the party in Gunnison would be busted, or become uninteresting before midnight and then they would head up to Crested Butte with hopes of finding some freaky, fun people to interact and party with.

"We've got to stop at the LQ," the Mountaineer said from the back of the Dolphin.

Hammer had already past the liquor store, but promptly did a U-turn in the middle of the road. "Ha, ha, I'm sober bitches," he said, imagining if he were to be pulled over by the local authorities.

Hammer was the first to walk into the liquor store. The employee at the register eyed him, and without hesitation pointed and said, "You're MC Hammer."

In this very moment, Rick was instilled with the utmost confidence that he was Hammer. There would be no more doubting. He was as excited as he could be as his friends picked out an assortment of beer and hard liquor.

Hammer drove everyone over to the house party, and the place was just as they expected, packed with mostly underage drunks. It was so insanely crowded that any movement in any direction meant you were going to touch someone. There was not near enough room to showcase their costumes and personalities. After less than an hour, Blow Up Doll stood up and announced, "Off to The Butte, and get your hands off my ass Cowboy."

Hammer took the wheel again. Once arriving in The Butte, they parked the car and out of nowhere the Million Dollar Cowboy pulled out a joint the size of Texas. What else were they to do? The Mountaineer was not up for this mountain of a joint, and quickly exited the Dolphin. The group barely noticed until fifteen minutes later when the Cowboy said, "I'm worried about Ed. He was pretty tore up, and you know how he gets. He'll drink a twelve pack and then go try and climb a mountain."

"But usually he barely gets to the base of it, and passes out in a drunken stupor," Blow Up Doll added. "Last Halloween we found some bears gnawing at his leg, after he passed out in a snow bank."

They exited the Dolphin in a way that could have been a scene out of any stoner movie, a cloud of smoke surrounding them. The cold night slightly altered their buzz. "It's so fricken cold," Blow Up Doll complained, his teeth chattering.

"Quit yer bitchin," the Cowboy responded using a Southern drawl.

"Please Cowboy, don't hurt the Blow Up Doll," Hammer said defensively, carefully altering words from a Hammer tune.

As the trio stumbled along Elk Avenue, the main strip of the small mountain town, Hammer realized his boom box wasn't working. They spotted the post office across the street, which was always open and warm. "Let's go in there and fix the box," Hammer directed.

Each had a forty ounce of Old English to chug before the bar and they attempted to fix the ghetto blaster. They thought of Ed, "Perhaps he's making a drunken attempt of Mt. Crested Butte," the Million Dollar Cowboy said, worried.

While speaking of Ed, drinking their 40s, and trying to fix the box, in walks Willy Wonka with a puzzled look on his face. He checked out the situation and without saying a word fixes the boom box. "It works, thank you Willy Wonka," Blow Up Doll said.

Hammer took a pull off the 40, hit play on the box, and along with Willy Wonka, the group hit the streets. "Now this is the scene," someone said.

"Yee haw, this is funner than skiing in jeans," the Cowboy hollered.

The boom box played a Hammer classic that the growing crowd recognized. Immediately the freaks in the streets of Crested Butte started an impromptu dance party. The crowd included: Nelly, Homer Simpson, Pamela Anderson, Salt-N-Pepa, Akeem from

Coming to America, Mike Tyson, polka dancers, Geraldo Rivera, Janet Jackson and Britney Spears. They all took to the Hammer vibe. It was as if the nineties never ended. Salt-N-Pepa were freaking with the Blow Up Doll between them and Nelly said, "It ain't hot in here, but it sure is fun."

The entrance to the bar they danced in front of, The Eldo, a famous Crested Butte bar, was so crowded that more and more people joined the party. "It's the Eldo Underground," Blow Up Doll yelled to the crowd.

"Ho," someone said.

As the tape slowed down to the Hammer love song, "Have You Seen Her?", Cowboy suggested they enter the bar via a cover free climb up to the deck of the bar. It was a climb more than one drunken patron had fallen off of and been injured on. To their surprise, they looked up to find an underage friend, the only person around without a costume on, quickly scale up the wooden pole that led up to the deck. He nearly fell when he reached a patch of snow near the top, but he pulled through.

Just as the Million Dollar Cowboy was about to start up, he looked at the ground and saw Ed's headband. "He must be in the Eldo," Cowboy said happily. By the time he'd realized this, a cop car rolled up alongside the group, wondering what was going on. "Just a little dance party, Mr. Policeman," Hammer offered quickly.

"Hey Cowboy, Blow Up Doll, we better be legit and pay the cover," Hammer said to his friends.

Inside the bar was entertaining, and the patrons had their wits about them more than the crowd at the house party in Gunnison. Quickly everyone noticed Michael Jackson, and they were all surprised when *she* entered the women's bathroom. Others might have been surprised to see the Blow Up Doll enter the men's room.

On the floor of the bar they found one of The Mountaineer's gloves, but no sign of him. Michael Jackson, straight out of the *Thriller* days, had some good moves and Hammer asked her to join him on the dance floor. Hammer shuffled and Michael Jackson did the moonwalk until Hammer's girlfriend, dressed up in a jazzercise outfit showed up, "Damn, Hammer's gotta get some of that," he said.

Hammer then stood up on a barstool, as if to make some announcement to the crowd, but before he could say anything, 5.14 Gene, an eighties rock climber in spandex, stood up on the bar above him and screamed, "Let's get wild," a phrase uttered only on special occasions in The Butte.

The crowd went wild.

Madness of this sort continued until closing time. Hammer's friend Lil' Kev asked to borrow the boom box and told everyone to get out of the bar. He added that there would be a special show for them out on the streets.

Blow Up Doll suggested to Hammer, "Let's get the Eldo Underground going again."

"That's hype," Hammer responded.

"What the hell are ya'll talkin 'bout?" the Million Dollar Cowboy asked.

Hammer grabbed the boom box and went into the street, which like usual at two in the morning was free of traffic, save for a couple cop cars cruising back and forth. He triumphantly yelled to the crowd that was spilling out of the Eldo, "It's Hammer time."

Hammer went into his routine, shuffling, breaking, shaking, jumping and twisting his body; Blow Up Doll and The Million Dollar Cowboy danced too! The Cowboy looked damn good doing his thing to the Hammer groove. A cowgirl quickly noticed him and danced close to him. Blow Up Doll had to fend off multiple drunken guys, who mistook him for a woman.

Before long, a crowd of fifty surrounded Hammer as if he were the real thing. Rick's mind drifted to his experience as a child seeing MC Hammer in the Mall of America. A chill went down his spine. This very moment was the ultimate goal of Halloween.

"You got to pray, just to make it today," another Hammer classic came on. Out of nowhere a man dressed up as Jesus showed up and held a bible in the air. An alien appeared which added to the strangeness. The crowd attracted people in costumes, which were being forced out onto the streets from neighboring bars. Even the police were watching and they were clearly enjoying it, with one cop even putting his hands in the air like he just didn't care.

Finally, after nearly the entire tape had played, the cops finally asked Hammer to disperse the crowd, "Hammer they love you. They won't listen to us."

Knowing the cops could've stopped it long ago, Hammer agreed if they let him have one more song. "This is the best night of my life," he told the cops, as he high-fived them and then high-fived the Million Dollar Cowboy and the Blow Up Doll.

The last song was Dancing Machine, and Hammer could hardly believe it when a half naked Ed the Mountaineer, with lipstick all over his face appeared, and joined the dance party. The crowd was on both sides of Hammer forming a dance line that he busted his best moves through. Then Hammer told the crowd he had to leave.

After continuing the show down Elk Ave for a while with Blow Up Doll, The Cowboy and three jazzercise girls, the group knew that Halloween was coming to a close. Now that's as much as I can recall, a tale that I'll admit may be altered by time and memory a little. But I'd say believe more of it than not. As Hammer would say,

"That's word because you know."

13 WILD TOM MALLY

In the kitchen at Donita's Cantina, where Tom Mally has spent twelve years slinging beans and rice, he is hurried and focused. He runs across the spacious kitchen mumbling to himself, while he prepares Mexican grub with his fellow cooks.

When the pace is fast he is all business, but when things slow down, he opens up, cracking jokes and telling stories of wilderness adventures. If you've worked at Donita's awhile, you may have already heard a version of the story. At forty nine years old, Tom has rambled from various mountain towns and has settled in Crested Butte, Colorado, attracted by its quietness and the lack of people.

A child of the east, he was raised in Long Island, New York. Tom also spent much of his teens living in Ireland. At seventeen, he wanted to see the country and hitchhiked out west.

"I hitchhiked across the country for six dollars," he says with pride. "One time I got stuck in Illinois for two days with no ride. Some guy stopped, and his car smelled like wine and beer. I didn't care; after two days waiting you'll get in the car with anyone."

Tom talks of sleeping on the cement beneath underpasses along the highway. In the Midwest, a moving truck picked him up and offered work. As they approached Denver near the end of the day, he remembers, "a sunset that looked like there were a zillion colors: green, blue, red, violet. I was hooked on Colorado from that point on."

After this summer, he returned east, but soon went back to the west. "I wanted to live like a hobo," he says.

Tom went out to the mountains near Flagstaff. "I had books on edible plants, a sack of flour and sugar, and a painter's cloth as a tent. I thought things like a tent and a sleeping bag were cheating."

The elements were rough on Tom. He lost thirty pounds, and at one point, got so thirsty he drank muddy water out of some tire tracks. As fall grew into winter, he watched the snow get closer and closer to his campsite. During an intense snowstorm, he decided it was time to leave. As he was leaving the wilderness, battling the snow, a guy who was bearded and skinny, looking like Cat Stevens, popped out of nowhere. "He looked at me and asked, *hey man*, you looking for Jesus?" Tom says.

In Flagstaff, someone gave Tom a peanut butter and jelly sandwich, "I spent three hours eating it. It was the most delicious thing I'd ever tasted."

Out of money and food, he returned to the east, living with his sister in upstate New York. That season was rough for Tom. He was drinking heavily, serving sub sandwiches to mean drunks on a graveyard shift. For him, the cruelty of humanity far exceeded the punishment that nature could deliver.

"In my life, the unfairness of human beings has been much worse than nature," he reflects.

Tom met his future wife in the east, and they moved into a trailer in Glenwood Springs, Colorado, "We didn't want to live in a damn city."

They lived there for a while and then moved to New Castle, Colorado, to a better, bigger trailer. During this era of his life, married and later with a child, he stopped any wild excursions and worked around the clock.

A divorce led him to living out of his truck and guerilla urban camping. During this time, he worked in a variety of restaurants in Aspen, Glenwood Springs and Redstone. He estimates he's cooked in fifty different establishments over the years.

Music was a big part of his life, too. Tom plays keyboards,

harmonica, clarinet, oboe, and the tin whistle, an instrument he learned to play while living in Ireland. In Aspen, he played in various bands, making some money, but now only plays music for the sake of playing music.

He liked the vibe of towns like Aspen and Vail before they were heavily developed, "I used to love those places," he says. "But they turned into something I didn't like."

Their crowding led him to Crested Butte in the mid-nineties, where his love for nature has grown. In Crested Butte, Tom enjoys camping, mountain climbing, biking and fishing. His approach to these typically doesn't involve motorized vehicles (he doesn't own a car) and he often partakes in the adventures solo.

What he calls the hidden hobo world has also fascinated him, and like in Flagstaff, the environment in Crested Butte has nearly killed him. For two winters, Tom camped out in the woods surrounding Crested Butte, one up Slate River and another up Kebler Pass. To some this may sound like a nightmare, but to Tom it is just the way he likes to experience life.

"Condensation is your worst enemy in winter camping in the Butte," he says. "And I always slept in a tent. I heard too many stories about snow caves collapsing on people."

"One night it got over thirty below zero; my eyes froze shut and my head froze to the pillow," he says with a smile. "I didn't dare fall asleep that night."

After his second winter, which he comments was easier than the first, he decided, maybe he was getting too old for this.

When asked about his opinion on the recent crackdown of campers surrounding Crested Butte, he is compassionate, but has come to the realization that people can't camp out in big numbers out there or it ruins the land.

He doesn't exclude the possibility of camping out again, and jokes that the authorities would have to find him first.

Though he does not face himself to the brutal cold of the dead of the winter, it's still not uncommon to hear about a Tom adventure, like the time he bought a townie bike in Gunnison and then proceeded to ride it thirty miles uphill to Crested Butte, facing the notorious headwind on a chilly fall evening.

For an adventurer that is approaching fifty, who has lived his life from one excursion to the next, from paycheck to paycheck, what does the future hold for Tom Mally?

"Good question," he answers. "And you know what, until recently, I hadn't really thought about it much. After my divorce, I didn't really care if I lived or died. But now I am glad to be alive. Kay Peterson-Cook, who runs Donita's with her sister Heli Mae, has really made me think of the future. She's brought me into the real world."

Kay considers Tom not only an employee of hers, but a good friend. "He is one of the backbones of this restaurant, and he's been rock solid for us in the kitchen," she shares. "I don't know if we could run Donita's without him, and I know we wouldn't want to."

In a town where restaurant employees change like revolving doors from the front of the house to the kitchen, she can't remember a time where he didn't show up for work in twelve years.

"I need to live in a small town with mountains, and I need some money," Tom says somberly. "I am not proud, I'll even wash dishes," the cook of over thirty years adds. "I look at it as this cosmic joke, that I've ended up working in a Mexican restaurant when French cuisine is the closest to my heart."

Tom looks at his life and notes the similarities with Christopher McCandless, the character in Jon Krakauer's famous *Into the Wild* novel that died of starvation in the wilderness in Alaska. "I think my feelings are the same as his. He was fed up with his existence and his family, and wanted to get out close to nature. I could have easily ended up like he did."

"I'm just a product of my generation, which was all about being a free spirit and adventuring," he adds.

Five days a week Tom can be found in the kitchen of Donita's, putting in overtime every pay period. In the busy season, he will run around, working hard so that the job gets done right. As things slow down, more stories and jokes will be told, some perhaps with certain elements added and taken away.

As our nation has become fascinated with the *Into the Wild* story, and continues to analyze why a bright young man died out in the Alaskan wilderness, here in Crested Butte there is a man who made similar mistakes but continues to live.

He is here for quietness, open space, to accept nature as it is, and to be away from the overcrowding of humans. One day he may leave the Gunnison Valley, but for now he is here, not because of money or luxury, but because he is still following an American dream, perhaps a version born of his generation, to live wild and free.

A version of this story was originally published in the Crested Butte Magazine, Winter 2008-2009.

14 REAL MOUNTAIN PEOPLE

"Dammit all the world is real and everybody carries on like it is a dream, like they were themselves dreams…pain or love or danger makes you real again."

Dharma Bums by Jack Kerouac

What is a real mountain person? This is essentially the question John Fayhee, the editor of the *Mountain Gazette*, posed to me in an email. Since then it's been lots of thinking, writing, throwing away (recycling), thinking, and here I am again, writing.

I've come to the conclusion I am both unable and unwilling to define what a real mountain person is. The main reason is that if I wrote about what a real mountain person is, I'd be saying that certain people who live in the mountains aren't authentic. Who am I to judge who belongs in a mountain town?

I am a typical example of a mountain town resident. I moved to Colorado from the Midwest and I've been here for most of the last seven years. Maybe if I was born and raised in the mountains, I could qualify to write about real mountain people. If I was a miner who lost his job and watched Crested Butte, where I'm writing from, turn from a mining based economy to a tourist based one. If I was a cowboy who suffers through the seasons year after year, through all the trials and hardships the mountains invite. Or if I was a Ute who lived off the land in the mountains only to have it developed by the white person, descendants who later put "native" stickers on their cars.

I am just another white guy who moved to the mountains with little, except hopes of finding something to live for, which the flatlands didn't seem to have for me. The search was for real mountain experiences, something I found through the enthusiasm and wonder of youth, the luck of being in the right place at the right time, and the often underrated advantage of having relatively little money.

Here is a little more about the message from Fahyee. In the email, he mentioned that he was moving from his home in the High Country of Colorado to New Mexico. One of his reasons, he stated, was people moving to the High Country didn't seem like real mountain people.

Now I think I know the kind of people he's talking about. Here's a semi-reasonable stereotype: they drive shiny vehicles, they are interested in real estate, and they usually come to the mountains with capital. These folks are flocking to Crested Butte, too.

In the last couple years, I've witnessed real estate prices skyrocket, and more flashy vehicles driving around. I could go off on the capitalists ruining mountain towns, but again who am I to judge? Have you ever heard the phrase, "Don't hate the player, hate the game?"

Besides, this game doesn't interest me. I feel the true wealth of mountain living lies in getting out there, in the hills and growing spiritually from these experiences. Out there, in my little campsite a couple miles out of town, where I'd easily surpassed the fourteen day limit. This was mountain living: a fire pit, a tent, boulders all around, the sweet smell of sage, birds a chirpin' and bunnies a hoppin'. I felt richer than any man in a mansion. No rent, no TV, no sofa, just a man and his thoughts. The plan went well till my car broke down. But what did I care? I had a bike, and two feet. During this experience, I found a peace of mind I hadn't experienced since I was a child at camp, in the woods. It was also a blessing as a young writer to have the stillness of silence every night, with the fire as my only entertainment. I experienced a magical moment, I can still vividly recall years later, sitting by the fire, a poem inspired by my surroundings, actually writing itself.

My friend Brent Armstrong is a little more out there than I am.

He was a guru to all us youngsters interested in the simple character building endeavor of rock climbing. He had his eyes on a prime piece of real estate down in the Black Canyon, an unclimbed big wall route. He spent nine days alone on the wall. I'd discovered living simply in the wilderness brought great thoughts and meditations, but living on a wall, what would that be like?

I never had the nerve to do a big wall climb alone, but I did get stuck on a wall overnight down in The Black. Dave Marcinowski and I didn't intend to spend the night on a cramped ledge, with barely enough room for the two of us to sit, a thousand feet above the Gunnison River, but I'm glad we did. We were essentially naked to the night, to nature. Having everything removed from your life makes one appreciate even the most basic things we many times take for granted. We asked each other questions like, "If you could have anything in the world what would it be?"

"Water, some food and a woman," was the answer.

Another buddy, Zach Alberts, is a simple cat, an inspiration to mountain town bums. The guy hasn't paid rent in like seven years, and he's one of the most pleasant individuals you'll ever come across. One summer, he set up camp amongst the local boulders, ones that happen to be in close proximity to a country club with multi-million dollar homes. If the owners only knew, there was this climbing bum living in the same setting, with the same mountains to view, with nothing but his tent and some food, content as could be. I wonder if the millionaires, burdened by their worldly possessions, are truly as happy as he is.

Tom Mally is another local I admire. I could camp out for six months in the warm seasons, but he camped out for two winters, this in a place that gets so cold many residents can barely afford their heating bill. I told him recently I admired him for his winter camping skills. He told me it wasn't so bad, and once he figured out how to stay warm, he really enjoyed the experience.

I think in America there is an illusion that having a lot of money will certainly provide one with a rich life. There is a freedom, a feeling, a lifestyle out there that can be lived without a lot of money. There are many ways to find this freedom, but, personally, I found this lifestyle by moving to a mountain town and learning from the people here.

After all these years, I still get this blissful feeling when I'm out there on a rock, in my tent, or with my friends, a feeling that is real, the thought that I should try to live more simply in order to find more happiness.

Out there, I also have this feeling deep inside in some way I owe the Natives who lived here before me, the miners who saw their way of life give way to the easier, but more complicated tourist based way of life, and the cowboys who still ranch on land that was once worth little and now is worth millions; the real mountain people who led the way for us living here now.

This piece was previously unpublished, but was submitted to the Mountain Gazette, circa 2006.

15 NAKED DISCO DANCE PARTY IN J-TREE

It is two o'clock in the afternoon on a warm spring day in the desert. "There's a naked disco dance party tonight," Holly says. Normally naked and party could be inviting, but in the climbing world the chances of a decent ratio of sexes is slim.

I've chosen the climbing life for the winter, a season that in J Tree, at times, can feel like summer. Living the dream, camping next to a brown government sign that reads "14-day camping limit." I'm not past that limit, no sir.

"Write and climb," is my answer for the usual, "So what do you do?" Of course I also wash dishes at Crossroads, the main social hub, the dusty little café and pub in the heart of town, to stay fed. It is all for the moments with friends in the sun on the perfect salt and pepper granite, climbing and observing the shenanigans of other climbers.

The climbers who come and go are interesting enough, but the ones who stay, who try to find ways to keep themselves entertained, are the best. Picture people who climb in superhero outfits, and surf atop Winnebagos driven through camp by their unsuspecting owners. These folks are the best campfire storytellers, and after two months, you've probably already heard one of Shoney's stories about the local heroes, narrated with eyes wide, hands and feet in the climbing position, "And then Too Strong Dave…"

I've heard that some of these folks have lived in Joshua Tree for years, while others have been hiding in the desert since the fall. Though I've shared a campfire with a couple of them and seen others run through camp midday dressed in costumes, most of the long staying freaks are a mystery to me. I've seen their headquarters, an incognito campsite where music, substances and partying seem to be of equal importance to rock climbing.

Now it's early evening and I am in my tent, in the routine, intending to get a good night's sleep for strong training tomorrow. Then I hear the loud, obnoxious voices, "Disco party tonight, meet at campsite 17." They grow louder, then softer, circling camp.

And then a female voice, "I'm going to take my shirt off."

A male voice, "Don't do it. You'll just attract more dudes."

An hour later, I look out of my tent as the rhythmic grooves of disco and funk float through the dusky air. Headlamps and unidentified glowing objects flash from atop The Blob, a hundred foot granite dome. Sleep is out of the question. I stagger amidst the bushes and boulders, drawn towards the lights.

The party isn't exactly easy to get to. Soon, I find two others tromping around in the bushes and boulders, one with the brightest headlamp on the market. With one sentence, "You trying to get up there, too?" we become a team.

The heathens above notice our lights, but aren't giving any help as to how to reach them. "Go up The Surrealistic Pillar," they taunt from above, suggesting we free solo a difficult 5.10 hand and face climb.

Our international team of three: myself, a fellow from Switzerland, and a guy from Sacramento, try to find a route up to the party. We locate an easy crack on the backside, one that swallows your hand with each jam.

"Did I tell you I've never climbed a rock before?" our Sacramento friend says in fear.

We try giving a lesson but don't want to encourage much

risk taking to the newbie. A fall here would send him and his backpack full of beer tumbling a hundred feet into boulders and cactuses. He retreats.

We reach the top, our bare feet adjusting to the rough granite. The stars are a backdrop and my soon to be friends are all naked, save for a hemp necklace here, or some flip flops there. A small stereo plays seventies disco.

"Welcome to the party, man," a six foot tall, naked dreadlocked man says. I have seen him around, climbing and camping.

I scan the ten naked people. No surprise, only two girls, one a dreadlocked free spirit they call The Mayor. This girl has been kicked out of the park over and over again, but slips back in. The Mayor is twirling some magical balls on a rope that change from yellow to green to red to blue in an instant. With a sweet look of innocence only a nude girl in California could give, she offers them to me to try, and encourages me to get naked.

Now I am amid the obnoxiousness, the openness, the idea to embrace the night, surely pissing off the climbers whose tents and fires look like specks in the low, far background. Then someone declares assertively, "Let's do the Chasm."

What the hell is the Chasm? I am clearly the only one thinking this, as the rest of the crew dances some more, puts on their clothes and down climbs off The Blob in different directions.

I get dressed and a walk off leads right to a fire in camp. Most people are naked again. The camp belongs to two tough looking biker dudes, one who says he is recovering from a wreck. One of my new friends is now wearing a bunny outfit, another has a curly blond wig on. Soon The Mayor busts out two torches. The torches shed a new light, as a crazier, wilder glow illuminates in the freaks' eyes. Beats from a Congo drum, thump, thump, indicate the party still has a pulse.

The next thing I know, I'm the only clothed person running through camp. People are screaming, announcing the trip to the Chasm, trying to round up others to be part of this clan.

Someone questions why I have my clothes on. "This event needs to be recorded," I claim, thinking if a ranger shows up I'll be happy to have something on.

"Well, if there's one thing we learned from Hunter S. Thompson, it was to participate," he answers, and adds with a direct look into my eyes, "Gonzo!"

Naked again, I am entering a chimney, burrowing into a granite cliff, away from the moonlight into pure darkness. "The chasm of doooom," someone yells, words echoing into the cave.

Move by move, beta is shared through the chimney, climbers tunneling, squeezing and down climbing; we pass a half an hour with no headlamps, only the shared word from above in the long tunnel up and then down through the granite rock. I wonder, where are we going?

Then we emerge, at a ledge, exposed and interwoven in a granite world, one where the stars are comforting, a tribe of tattooed naked climbers. Smoke pours from mouths, cold air blows through on our skin. We look out onto the endless granite and Joshua trees, each their own shape, with every limb going its own direction, barely visible by the moonlight.

Down climbing the chasm is horrible, the scraping skin, claustrophobic thoughts in the dark world. My mood lightens for a second when someone says, "Watch your package here."

Just when I've had enough, there's an opening: the sand, the boulders, the cacti, the horizontal world. We run again to camp on the road, no cars, only the pat of bare feet on pavement, and inhalations and exhalations. The bunny leads, fire torches behind her, dreads flying through the air. If the law were to drive by, it could be bad.

We arrive in camp. The crew, through inspiration or annoyance, has invited me into their group. I look up to The Blob; granite clearly lit up by the moon is stunning. Camp is completely quiet. My tent, weathered badly by the wind, poles sticking through the nylon, begs me to enter in it, to another dream.

A version of this story was originally published in Rock and Ice, issue 170.

16 HOME IS WHERE THE CLIMBING IS

Last year it was Mexico I was intimidated by crossing the border, this year it is the United States. We'd been climbing in Mexico for a month, two Gunny climbers, who realized how much we liked the warm weather over the brutal cold of Gunnison, Colorado.

Our trip had been loosely planned by a handful of buddies almost immediately after our voyage down there the year before, but just Scott and I ended up showing.

Crossing back to the States into Texas, the border patrol is suspicious of me, especially when I answer that I am a writer when he asks me what my occupation is. "Let me see your work," he says authoritatively.

I look in my book bag and carefully choose the notebook that doesn't have pot leaves drawn on it. It is the start of a book.

"What is your goal in life?" he asks.

"Uh, I guess to travel and climb till I have a wife and kids," sometimes you even surprise yourself when you say something.

"You're gonna have a heck of a time providing for a family just climbing around and traveling."

United States, land of the hassle, I think.

Mexico was so mellow and friendly, especially out in the hills.

I've seldom felt the purpose I felt the last month climbing there. Many people look at the climbing bum lifestyle and see it as just escaping reality. But it is very meaningful for the mind, the body and the soul. And if you're a young man full of testosterone, it keeps one relatively out of trouble. Scott Borden, my climbing partner, added purpose to the trip, as each climb we did raised money for cancer prevention and awareness through his Climbing for a Cause and a

Cure fundraiser, which he did this past winter-spring across the globe, with sponsors from The States. We ended up completing one hundred pitches, and saw a rattlesnake while rappelling, during the final climb.

I suppose it's the negative vibrations that scare me, but it's more than that. It's that many Texans seem to want everything so big, they consume so much, but for some reason many times don't seem to be as happy as the Mexican who has little, but family.

I miss Mexico the minute I am across the border. But like many times before in my life, hope for America is renewed by our young; my good friends Bennett and Ashleigh, who recently moved to Austin from Crested Butte, Colorado to further pursue their education, and study sustainable architecture. A move I admire, as I'm still daydreaming and road tripping not really doing much in the movement to make the world a better place. I work as much as necessary, and then I dirtbag it and play.

I stay with them for a few days, but after awhile on the couch and doing the city thing, I become restless. This domestic life isn't for me. I've got to get back to climbing.

After the twenty hour marathon drive back to Colorado, I stop in Gunnison. From Highway 114, I remember the cold of the Gunny winter. It makes me sad. However, it's the people there that matter. The cold makes me want to drive right through to the Moab desert, but I stop, of course, because Gunny is home and even when you are on the road searching, living out the freedom of your youth, one needs a home.

For a moment I felt at peace, because Duffy and I got out to Taylor Canyon, and for a couple hours, it was pleasant. Then it snowed, and I remembered why I left for the winter.

The next day with Shane and his two broken hands, and Adam,

a friend just visiting Gunny, we end up at one of Gunnison's sketchy bars; smoky and full of faces I recognize from many years past still living out their Sundays in this dump. What else are we to do? It's cold and Shane is all broken. The PBR that we drink, and the Grateful Dead blasting from the jukebox are strangely comforting, and for only one day, it's not too destructive, yet another reminder why I left Gunnison for the wintertime.

The next morning it's off to Moab, to the red rock sandstone desert, Indian Creek. Winter is quickly forgotten. The climbing life there is like anywhere else, living in the dirt. After a month, the red dirt is in *everything*, it crunches in your teeth when you eat, it is on your clothes, and in your sleeping bag.

I climb with old Gunnison friends. We are able to forget that time has separated us, and we are united again through climbing. To tie in with a friend on a rope, a connection that we'll share till we're dead, to spend time away from civilization in the desert, it clears the mind, opens it to dreaming. To dream to climb something that long ago was so difficult, on the verge of impossible. Like the tower that Mark and I climbed. Four hundred feet tall, climbed by its cracks, a hundred feet up I was calling for retreat, mostly because of a large death block that I would've had to climb around.

Mark went up anyways and checked it out, carefully climbing around the death block, which easily weighed a couple hundred pounds. The crack was dirty and dusty, and I watched my friend magically and carefully execute the moves. Damn, he's been skiing in Crested Butte all winter, and I've been climbing, I thought. I should have been able to lead that. Climbing is forever humbling. And occasionally successful.

Success! What a feeling. Even its success from this contrived game derived from mountain climbing that is modern rock climbing.

And the stories to tell.

Of the horses that trampled my new tent, crushed my beer, knocked over my cooler and all of my water, when water is sixty miles away round trip, what heartache!

Of running into the main strip of campsites with the hope of finding a climbing partner for my last day of climbing, getting into the trance of the desert, cherishing every hill, every rock tower, each black bird in the sky.

Running as the sun set slowly and seeing Steve appear from his campsite, a Gunny friend who last I knew quit climbing after a big fall in an avalanche ice climbing. It was like he was a mystic mirage. But there he was back to climbing, back to the dream.

When I return to Gunnison on the heels of summer, the twists and turns of the drive are exciting and Gunny seems full of new hope. The snow is melting, the sun is out and the sky is that pure blue. I go straight to the bar, and of course there are familiar faces, some friends excited to see me, others act like they just saw me yesterday. The freshness of being back won't last long, probably only last till I've seen each friend for the first time since returning. Home is home and everyone needs to have a home. Plus there is plenty of inspiration in this valley to plan for next winter.

A version of this piece was originally published in The Gunnison Valley Journal, seventh edition.

CLIMBING OUT OF BED

17 CLIMBING OUT OF BED

It was summer in The Rockies and love presented itself, as if the answer to a dream. Later, lust made its appearance, confusing everything, and as the summer was unwinding, I felt compelled to let the women of my summer fade into memory, and drift towards friendship and nature and climbing.

The climbing life is like poetry. Being somewhat removed from this existence with the demands of steady employment, I sometimes forget the feeling, the clarity the mind finds after a long, hard climb, the satisfaction of living very close to nature, and the bond that grows out of trust and sweat between climbing partners. With that in mind, I set off from the Gunnison Valley, Colorado, into a great expanse that separates us from another holy, sacred place, Yosemite Valley, California.

The women of life, I can't live without them and really I was never given a choice. They (or you) are poetry too, but sometimes too exhausting and consuming. This summer in particular was draining to my heart. The first love was real and honest, yet with a woman whose scars from life damaged her in a way that our love could not continue without constant drama. The second love of the summer, the lust, hit me down below, and thoughts of her dominated my psyche and left me unable to have a meditative state of mind. By the time we were hitting the road, my soul was crying out for the clearing and cleaning that climbing provides best.

It was a tremendous coincidence that my good friend and summer couch surfer Brian was driving to Yosemite the very day that my summer vacation was set to start. I was nearly broke, so the couch surfing karma was important; I knew Brian would let me catch a lift without paying for much gas. Brian would be staying at his new home in Santa Rosa, California, so I could look forward to a slow train ride back home for reflection.

I like Brian for many reasons, and on a cross country journey, I knew he'd be infinitely entertaining. He's one of those people who's always verbalizing most of his thoughts, so conversation could go anywhere from sustainable building to the little Seinfeld like scenes we all go through in life. He's an engineer who has worked as a timber framer, who also enjoys taking three months at a time off from work, hence the couch surfing. Since he's always talking, he always makes me think. This notion was confirmed when he wholeheartedly agreed that we should bring a dictionary along on our journey, to test each other's vocabularies. He also thought it was a great idea to do twenty pushups every time we stopped and got out of the truck, my kind of guy.

Just over a hundred miles west, we left my car in the Grand Junction train station parking lot. Fifteen hours to go till Yosemite. Leaving Colorado into Utah is always about stepping out of the comfort zone. Seeing that Leaving Colorful Colorado sign, sometimes I can't help but wonder if I will return alive, those thoughts are followed by the comfort that even if I don't return living, my friends, ones I know and ones I've yet to meet, will continue on in the path of climbing and friendship and all that comes along with that.

When we couldn't drive any more we slept. We ended up in a town, close to Yosemite, where there was coffee, groceries and climber looking people. I was barely surprised when I saw a climber we knew from the Gunnison Valley in the coffee shop. "Yeah, I've been out here in California for awhile now," he said in that California way. "It got a little too cold over in Crested Butte."

The climbing community stretches from sea to sea, offering endless couch surfing and opportunities for fun and fitness, a culture and economy of its own. Back in Gunnison there is this apartment complex called the Cebolla Lodge. In my twenties, I lived there, camped out in the front yard in a tent, made love there, argued with the landlord and watched friends pass through on their journeys. It was a basecamp of sorts.

Our connection in Yosemite was Mark, who was living the dream more than any other rock climber I knew. I can't help but wonder if his experiences in his college days at Western State in Gunnison shaped his psyche and his attitude towards living for the moment. During his senior year, he was diagnosed with testicular cancer, which led to surgeries, radiation treatment and finally chemotherapy. During this entire time, he remained a climber, surprising the hell out of more than one friend when he'd asked to stop at a climbing area on the way back from the five hour round trip for radiation treatment. Then he'd climb his way to the top of some difficult crack route, and many times the friend could not even repeat the route that he'd just completed.

He's also Brian's best friend from childhood. Brian once told me a story of Mark climbing in the gym after a chemotherapy treatment. Mark was trying his damnedest to climb up a vertical wall with small holds, grunting and giving it his all. As innocent, young and dumb climbers will do, a bystander started yelling unsolicited beta (information) about the climb up to Mark, a pet peeve to many a traditional climber, "Put your left hand up to that crimp, move your right foot up to the hold with red and white tape…"

Mark, bald from the chemo, dangling from the rope, could have responded, "Shut the fuck up," but he simply yelled back in frustration, "You don't understand. I'm on chemotherapy."

Four years later and still cancer free, he's settled into a life of a rock climbing guide. He also enjoys leisurely stretches between work by traveling, couch surfing, skiing, yoga, and he's even picked up surfing, not only couches, but actually waves of the ocean. On a recent climbing trip, he met Norma, an architect from Mexico. Norma had joined him in California, where Mark had somehow secured two hundred dollars a month rent at some prime real estate in Yosemite. When he's homeless, an old camper on top of his Ford truck works as home.

Mark told me that he was living in the best house in Yosemite, and he's not one to hype up things that aren't great. We rolled into The Green House, slightly haggard from our travels, and ready for some rest. It was midday and late summer, hot and humid, nearly oppressive. I took refuge on their trampoline under a tree and drifted off to sleep.

The house wasn't the greatest because it fit into a definition of luxury; it was the greatest because of the location and rustic feeling. It was a mere ten minute drive from the famous glaciated granite walls for climbing, the floors creaked when you walked on them, the kitchen had a bucket of water under the sink that constantly needed to be changed as water was used, and there was no bathroom, only an outhouse.

Later, I began to learn the stories of The Green House. It was another basecamp, hundreds had stayed within its doors, and the journals in the living room recorded this. They brought the place alive, all the way from its rustic roots of being farmland and a stop along the way for the railroad, to the current role of housing outdoor educators and couch surfers passing through Yosemite.

Our story, our climbing, well, it was hot in Yosemite, so much so that there were not any other climbers there, and essentially we had the most famous walls of the United States to ourselves. Once the mileage and toil of the road wore off, I began to feel free and content, I was here to climb them walls, and when we weren't climbing, there was food and beer, and there were the people who make this climbing life worth living.

There was some structure to our days; I would fall asleep on the trampoline and then awaken later to the coyotes howlin' in the middle of the night. The sun was the natural alarm clock, but hitting the snooze button of the heat was impossible. Mark was off to the park in the morning to work nearly every day. If he didn't work, we would climb; if he did, we would climb later after he was off.

Some climbers used to call Yosemite the center of the universe. It is the most popular big wall climbing area in the world. It also sees millions of tourists from all over the world. In mid August it was busy, like a city, while the daunting granite walls and small trickles of waterfalls stood above it all.

I was looking for release, and it was coming. Haunted by the desires of the flesh from the woman that I lusted for but did not love, I began to forget about her by being immersed in the day to day meditations of living for climbing. Like all women, from the ones that have broken my heart, to the ones that simply fulfill my urges, she slowly faded into memories. After the fiendish feelings from the previous weeks, I was pleased that my consciousness and body were content with the simple life.

Mark, Norma and I hiked up to the Cookie Cliff. The objects of our desire were some crack climbs, ones that went for a hundred or two hundred feet, practice climbs for the big walls that always lay ahead in dreams. Norma let us go. I suppose if you are going to date a climber, you must let them go. Norma was the coolest, *tranquillo*. We just went and she stayed content at the base of the walls.

Somewhere in climbing, the past fades; the voice in your head moves on from rewind or fast forward, and the poetry begins. My memory comes in when I began leading, which basically means you're climbing with the rope placing gear in as you go, so you fall and when you fall you go until your protective gear stops you. The knotted stomach and butterflies compares to asking someone out that you really dig.

I reached into my chalk bag, and powdered up my sweaty hands, jammed my fingertips into the crack, the tips of my shoes barely going in; it's an instinctual thing, climbing, a flow and a pace is developed by measuring fear, fitness and fun. More or less for forty feet now, three hundred feet above the towering pine trees below, I'm moving up the perfectly vertical, straight up rock, looking for anything on the side of the crack, dime sized edges to stand on with my feet. I place cams into the crack, a rush surging through my body as I pull up the rope to clip in. I'm working as hard as I can, the limit, when I reach up to slide the tips of my fingers into the crack, and I pop off falling fifteen feet in a split second weighting the rope, with a scream that echoes into evening, something primal. I get back on, and keep climbing.

Norma seems content when we return, rappelling down the granite face shouting nonsense loudly in the air because we can, because we like the feeling of yelling jokes that only we get. The language barrier between Mark and Norma enhances their true communication of love.

At dinner, over soy sausages, we explain some English slang to Norma. Somehow we talk about love, and all the slangs and directions that love could take. She says quietly to Mark, "I love you," with no idea of how sincere and poetic she was.

"Living's mostly wastin' time," a lyric in a song by Townes Van Zandt I used to listen to all the time. I guess I wasted a lot of time on that trip. Climbing demands rest to build those muscles and to be psyched on pulling your body up the granite cliffs day after day. So I'd just walk around there, feeling some yin and yang attraction, and looks from women with their summer aura about them, as we were dwarfed by the towering granite walls, the blue sky above, the ninety degree heat, the trees and the deer and squirrels all running around. Eating ice cream for calories and energy, to stay cool, and when that didn't work, finding release in the river, which instantly energized and cooled off that oppressive August heat.

Our next memorable moment on the walls came a few days

later. I had to leave back for Gunnison to work soon, so we planned around Mark's schedule, and the energy that comes with the steady pace of conditioning with a bigger, physically demanding goal ahead. That goal became a thousand foot wall, which faced north, and got shade all day. Just opened to climbing after being closed for months to peregrine falcons and their nesting, it's called The Rostrum, and it finishes up as a hundred foot wide pinnacle, right at the top of a canyon, where beer and the car are right there. But I'm getting ahead of myself with thoughts of celebration and ending.

Mark was off work around four in the evening, so we only had about four hours of daylight left. The plan was to rappel down into the canyon, attempt to do the entire route in that remaining time, but if our ambitions were unrealistic, we could sneak off the wall via a simple escape with minimal trickery.

I'd heard of the route for years, even saw video of a man climbing it with ease, without a rope. It was always closed for the falcons that nest up there, or out of my realm because I wasn't strong enough on previous trips. I went into the thing a little cocky, thinking it would be vertical hiking. It was more like the master that is Mother Nature had to teach my consciousness a lesson. I wormed up a chimney to reach Mark's perch, as he belayed me up. We did the transfer of the gear, my mind not at all present; we had eight hundred some feet of rock towering above us, and the daylight was nearing an end. "I need progress," my ego said, "and I need it soon."

Confused by a rating on the topo, the piece of paper that described the route, the range of the rating made it seem well within my ability, and it was, but it was not vertical hiking, it was vertical finesse that was needed. The brain needed to be calm, the body needed to perform in a yogic way; the vertical terrain above me would demand everything I possibly had.

I was traversing on small edges again with my feet reading the rock for holds, trying to dance with the rock, but I wasn't dancing at all; I was tense, the mind demanded, "the clock is ticking." But no clock was ticking, the rock wasn't going anywhere, it would be patient, the err here within the form of the human. Since I wasn't dancing, wasn't using the yoga I had in me, I tried to muscle. Muscling it, I didn't correctly, strategically put my gear in the rock, an eighth of an inch crack was all there was. I climbed awkwardly with fear, putting my feet and hands in all the wrong places, my inner voice doubted, sent negative thoughts all around; I couldn't tell you for sure, but I bet my anus was gripped.

I relayed my fear and doubt to Mark, "I don't know man. Can you just do this? I just don't think I have it."

As patient as the rock, he refused to let me slip further into my spiral of doubt. "No, you've got it. You can do this." Kind words from a true friend.

I eventually struggled my way through it, not pretty, not dancing, but our journey continued. Of course, we took the mellow option, sneaking off the climb with perfect cracks above us for seven hundred more feet. But I was tired, humbled, just in need of food, and the rock above didn't inspire, but it would soon enough, the rock always inspires the climber. Love always comes back around if you believe in it, maybe not in the same place, but if you keep climbing up the hill, keep waking up with hope that with the new sunrise are new possibilities, you're bound to find that magic again. Climbing, athletic and masochistic, silly at times for a grown man to be infatuated with it, it's about love really, if you don't love it, and the experience, well, there are other things to do with your time.

I had a pizza dinner with my new favorite couple the night before returning to the climb again. I felt the love, no awkwardness being the third wheel. We talked like people talk when someone is about to leave. We explained more words to Norma, made plans to all meet up in Mexico over New Years. Norma would introduce me to all her friends. I'd get to keep working on my Spanglish.

It's a great feeling to be ready for the big climb. Proper conditioning, nutrition and attitude, when those things come together, the dangerous activity of climbing is joyous to share with your partner. You get out what you put in.

I woke up that morning and just had a good feeling in my mind and my gut. We leisurely got our things together, had a breakfast of soysauge and eggs, good protein, and visited with the newest arrivals to The Green House, Outward Bound instructors wrapping up their summer. There would be a small party, with more coming in tonight for beer and a bonfire, toasting to the end of the season.

We started late, not too late, just in time where we knew in our internal clocks of climbing experience that we could climb the thousand feet before it got dark. I asked Mark if I could lead the pitch that gave me such a mental battle before. He obliged. I knew he would.

I went into the climbing aware of the difficulty, the risk, not over gripping the handholds, carefully placing protection into the crack. Still the nervousness was in my stomach, but that's good, it lets you know you're alive. The move sliding my right hand pinky and ring finger barely into the crack then leaning left putting my weight on barely an inch of those fingers. I had pulled through. I was dancing. It was yoga, and positive vertical progress ensued.

The climb was the best ever because I had to try, really had to do, and I did. Mark, a Yosemite master, showed me his vertical walking, but still grunted in sections. Some of the climb demanded that in the moment precision with just the fingertips and edges of my shoes on the wall, other parts half my body chimney-ed in a crack, with my elbows and knees and feet making the slow upward progress.

It is the physically demanding climbing like this that requires the mind stay in the moment. The breaks in between, when you are sitting on a two by two foot ledge tending to the rope, waiting for your partner to join you, dangling a thousand feet above the river below, is when the mind spaces out and thoughts travel.

I often think at these moments of repose, where is she? The next woman in my life, the one that will make all the awkward dating worth it, the woman that I've convinced myself exists. The one that has to be alive and struggling in love just like me, the one I'll fall in love with, and I'll live from season to season with, finding intimacy and self awareness at an entirely new level. All the past lovers have given me great gifts, but past loves are like past climbs, they only exist in memory and don't add up to much. I wonder, where is she, and when will she be ready for me, and am I truly ready for her? I look off into the distance, dangling my feet off the cliff looking into the trees, up to the sky, and say the unspoken prayer of what I want out of the rest of my life in love.

The last pitch was one of those bigger cracks, where you have to figure out what side of your body to slide in for progress. It got so wide at one point I had no gear in; had I fallen it would have been a big disaster, a possible tumble fifty feet down the vertical rock.

Reaching the top of that crack, there we were, through the struggle. We shook hands, a team that had won, accomplished the goal. We were there, mentally, spiritually and physically.

The bonfire, beer drinking, party was full of outdoor educators who had wrapped up their seasons. The next morning folks would be off to Washington, Oregon, and the East Coast. On the phone, I tried to buy a last minute train ticket, only to find out they were working on maintaining the tracks between Utah and Colorado, I'd have to take a bus if I wanted to make it back for work on Monday.

The bus was less romantic than an old train, across the desolate strange vastness that connects the two valleys, Yosemite and Gunnison. It was painfully slow, but I had a high and a feeling of satisfaction from the climbing. Part of the frustration was that we had to go all the way down to Los Angeles, when the direct route was just to head east. But in L.A., when I got on the bus, a cool black fellow, asked me "What are you a base jumper or something?" when he saw my rope on my backpack. I thought he was making fun of me, but we went on to have the best conversation I'd ever had with a stranger. Normally I bury my head into literature or fade into my headphones to avoid awkward conversation.

He told me his background, of being a young drug dealer, who'd spent a lot of time in jail, of witnessing first hand killings in L.A. But he was a plumber now, who was into cars, and listened to any subject I wanted to talk about with sincerity. We talked about spirituality, of God, and he told me about his beliefs; I told him about mine. We talked about the power of prayer, and he told me that was why he believed in God. He told a story of his obsession with sex, and how he needed to move past it, how he could not focus or think of anything else; he prayed, and he was able to free himself from that bondage. I wondered if we were best friends in a past life, we looked deep into each other's eyes when we talked.

It was almost exhausting, the conversation. It was deep. I was relieved when he got off the bus to meet his woman. The bus ride went on forever. I listened to the same songs over and over on my MP3 player and looked at rolling hills and thought about where all the other occupants of the bus were going, with little interest of actually talking to them to find out.

After an eternity, the bus crossed over that wonderful Welcome to Colorful Colorado sign, I never grow tired of returning to see. I realized I'd survived another climbing trip, and that I was going home again, alive, and that it was the end of summer and the beginning of something.

I've slipped back into my 9-5 world, which is fine. I pay the bills and eat good food and have a roof over my head. I get to climb often and get to taste that feeling. We've got the Black Canyon here, our own Yosemite, even better in some ways, less crowded, more wilderness, and more pristine. A place, that if even for a day, the mind and body can forget the troubles of flesh and indulge in the magic that is called rock climbing.

I've learned a thing or two about what I want out of love. I want what Norma and Mark have. I want the desires of flesh to be met, but to have that happen also with love and not lust. I can't slip and give into the desires without it.

A couple months after returning, Dave, another kindred spirit and mountain guide, passed through Gunnison and stayed on my couch. Dave spends a great deal of time in the mountain climbing consciousness, months on Denali, the highest mountain in the United States, up in Alaska, and countless days on the rock in various western states. Over a beer we talked about what mountain guys, who are much softer on the inside than the outside talk about: climbing, the desire for home, and of course love. He'd met a woman that weaved into his intricate and delicate climbing life.

"You know," he said. "Women are the greatest thing on this planet."

I imagined Dave as a mystic searcher, like many climbers are, and all human beings have the potential to be. He's experienced the freedom of a thousand days in mountain environments. A freedom many of us only glimpse in television commercials and in the pages of *National Geographic*. He's been to the mountaintop and that was his gem to share to the valley below.

I thought about what he had to say, and I hoped on his next visit, that I would have a woman in my life to tell him all about.

18 A YEAR IN THE HEART OF A CLIMBER

"Some people say that love is a losing game. You start with fire and you lose the flame. I'll take my chances and I'll risk it all. I'll win your love or I'll take the fall."

You'll Accompany Me by Bob Seger

I believe I left off last time, concluding my essay by stating that women were the greatest thing on this planet. Well, women and climbing of course.

This past fall I'd just returned to the Gunnison Valley, Colorado, from a climbing trip to Yosemite Valley, California. It was one of those trips that made me feel optimistic about everything. I was in good shape, for myself. With climbing, it's all about your own standards and goals; trying to measure up to another's is a sure way to fail in the climbing path. I was also single, and a new season was about to unfold, the colorful and nostalgic autumn.

I met her on assignment for work, taking her photo as part of a story I was working on for the college. Yes, it was fall, she was dressed up nice, in one of those mountain woman Patagonia skirts that showed she belonged here in Gunnison, but also with a style in her hair and makeup that told me she came here from another place, perhaps the East Coast?

I didn't ask her out right away; I would have appeared too eager, plus it was a work assignment, and I needed to remain professional. We casually exchanged names, but I made a mental note that when I saw her again I would try to establish a connection.

The Gunnison Valley is great because it's small. Had I been in a city and met this beautiful, striking, young woman, I would have had to get her number, or at least a full name to look her up on Facebook, taking some romance out of the process. This beauty would stand out in Gunnison, and I knew it was only a matter of time before I'd see her again.

It happened in the Gunnison airport; I was about to board a plane back home to Illinois, when I saw her out of the corner of my eye. I purposely walked past the boarding area to strike up a conversation, acting like I'd ran into her by accident. She was waiting to pick up a friend from New York City, and I only got a few words in before her friend got off the plane, nearly tackling her with an energetic hug. I left to board my plane to the Midwest, all the while thinking of this new woman in town who had captured my imagination.

A couple weeks later, we were having coffee and trail running now and again. She had all the right qualities: good looking, smart, athletic and psyched on living in the mountains. Plus, there was a connection, and that feeling in my gut that I simply had to pursue her. A feeling that I could not stop, but one that took a sharp turn when it was revealed, she had a boyfriend back east.

When your heart tells you that something should be pursued, I believe you should listen to that, even if there will be suffering. I still wanted to pursue Lynn, but I'm not the type of guy who wants to date a girl with a boyfriend, nor would I want to date a girl with a boyfriend who would date someone else. I wrote in my journal to console myself, and poured my heart out to friends over beers. I'd known this woman for a mere few weeks, but I felt something, a strong feeling, that I simply had to pursue her.

So, where many lovers begin, to quote Common, I tried to focus on gaining her friendship. We hiked up Taylor Canyon one day, and then the following weekend, I convinced her to try climbing at Hartman Rocks. She was deathly afraid of it, and only would go after I promised her she would not die.

It was late fall by now, and a stunning day in early November. One of those bluebird days that feeds optimism and exercise, and creates a high that no drug could ever compare with. Hartmans would soon be snowed in and too cold for comfortable climbing. The grueling Gunnison winter was on its way with one last glimpse of the Indian summer for us to soak in.

She trusted me enough to do a climb on the Beginners' Slabs, shaking her way up the route, while constantly seeking reassurance that she was safe. She was. When she completed the climb and was lowered back to the ground, she reflected that because the experience was so terrifying it might be the one and only time she went rock climbing.

But she said something later, sitting on a rock, watching others climb, that was enough to plant a seed in my brain that I had a chance with her, someday, "This is the best day ever."

I found myself wanting to see more and more of Lynn. One morning we went for a run before work, even before coffee, and I decided when the run was over I was going to tell her how I felt about her.

With a bumbling nervousness, I started to express my thoughts and feelings. There was no reciprocation; she told me that she had a boyfriend and had to be loyal to him. For the rest of the day, I thought maybe my heart would just stop beating. I was anxious and wondered to myself if I should have kept those feelings inside.

It all changed once the truth in my heart was expressed. We stopped talking on the phone, sending emails and running. I didn't even try to take her climbing again; it was winter anyways, and we would have had to travel and camp in order to find some warm rock. On my birthday, in December, she agreed to have a cup of coffee with me. She told me that she couldn't spend time with me anymore. She had to remain faithful to her boyfriend. I walked out of the coffee shop, snow looked to be building in the clouds; it was time to settle into loneliness and winter.

Those who have lived through a Gunnison winter understand something about patience. They are long and cold. If you're a downhill skier or snowboarder, and it snows, it can be paradise. But that bug never bit me; I always find the winter in the Gunnison Valley to be the most difficult season to endure. Like I said before, climbing typically demands travel once it starts snowing in December till the temperatures break into the 40s in mid-March. And climbing is at the heart of my existence, something I rely on heavily for health, happiness and fitness.

I eventually tried to make peace with my feelings for Lynn; even though I wanted to be with her, there was nothing I could do except wait out her long distance relationship, or just let it go.

I wrote in my journal, *"There is a natural way that things happen. It would be foolish to plant a seed outdoors in the winter, silly to ski on a hill without snow. But just as I want to eat from the garden and smell the flowers, perhaps to have you I must just have to be patient and wait for the sun to come back around."*

I tried my best not to sink into the despair of the Gunnison winter, the time of year when I am the least active. I continued to run on the snowy trails nearby and tried to stay positive. A New Year's climbing trip was planned to Mexico, and I escaped with friends to Boulder to climb in one of their fancy gyms. I had a better attitude about the winter than ever before.

I thought of Lynn less and less; not that I didn't still desire her affection, I still did, but because I needed to move on. I still spoke with close friends about her, and my patterns of dating. I typically dated in the past when I was energetic and happy, in the months of spring, summer and fall. Sometimes the women of the summer would leave after their time ran up in the Gunnison Valley and they had to return east or south for school. Other times the natural rhythm of love would simply end once everything started freezing up. But I was slowly realizing that it was me who would freeze up and become inactive come winter.

So that winter I just tried to be active, and strive for health and fitness. The running really helped. A lunch break run, when it was a mere ten degrees outside, would make me feel alive and energized. I even joined the college's Cross Fit club, a new hybrid sport mixing cardio exercises with light weightlifting. My Cross Fit coach was Wallace, a friend I'd met the previous fall, who consoled me when I spoke to him about Lynn. I thought I was doing alright.

January and February passed, and soon it was March. Climbing season was just around the corner. When Spring Break came around I was off to warmer climates, to southwest Utah, with the simple mission of being warm for a few days and climbing a few routes. I met up with Wallace out there, and repaid his Cross Fit lessons, with some climbing lessons. Lynn had all but faded from my thoughts, and I figured she had probably forgotten about me as well.

On that mini climbing trip we sampled some sandstone sport routes near St. George, Utah. It was truly glorious to bask in the warm sun after the frigid Gunnison winter. We spent a couple days in Zion, and Wallace tried the brutal art of crack climbing for the first time. On the drive back, with the sun shining and spring on its way, I felt optimistic again.

The week after Spring Break, on a writing assignment, I was interviewing a professor, also a good friend, and was given some important news about Lynn, "Did you hear she's leaving to go back east, and…she broke up with her boyfriend."

The one-two punch of the news was dramatic. I wasn't surprised to hear she was leaving though; people come and go from the Gunnison Valley all the time. I didn't think that this news gave me much of a chance until I heard from her a couple weeks later in an email, "My friend from New York City is in town, would you like to get a drink with us this week?"

It ended up being the same friend that she'd been waiting for in the airport the day I ran into her. A small group of friends all went for a drink together after work, at the local wine bar. I made sure I sat next to her. A few moments into the conversation, I remembered that connection we had, and I made sure that plans were made to do something that coming weekend. We planned to go on a bike ride. When you're living in the mountains of Colorado, a bike ride might as well be the equivalent of living in the city and going on a first date.

On a walk, after the bike ride, she told me the story, and I acted like I didn't already know; she'd taken a job back east and broke up with her boyfriend. She was leaving, just as my chance was arriving. But in the mountains, the opportunities come and go quickly, like the chance to summit before a thunderstorm. I still had to take the chance to love this fine, young woman.

The mountain way of courting (biking, running, climbing) ultimately led to being invited over for a movie, and then it was natural for romance to ensue. After that winter, making love was like slipping into a hot spring away from the cold. I was completely content in the moment and never wanted it to end. Of course she made me wait just the right amount of time; men, I think it's in our DNA to always be ready, and we rely on the woman to say when.

We went to the hot springs, and did those things that lovers do in the spring, while living in the mountains, simple things, yet the most important things that young people should do, just simply enjoying love and being alive. I even loved her dog, a golden retriever that she rescued, that was the cutest, sweetest dog I'd ever seen. We ran and biked with the dog out in the hills. We went to yoga together. We shared everything we could and were both high on life and love. One day I told her those elusive three words, "I love you," something I'd never told another lover.

Things were incredible. My confidence was at an all time high, and I had everything in life I wanted. I gave little thought that soon, when summer started really rolling, she would be leaving back to the East Coast.

We were intoxicated on that loving feeling, but we still talked about her departure now and again. Since we liked each other so much, and I'd never felt that way about anyone, I thought she might be the one. I held the thought of continuing our relationship after she left as an option. For a brief, sweet period of time I could not even consider being with another woman. Perhaps my single mountain man days of loneliness were coming to an end.

Adventures led us to try out more climbing together. She really trusted me now and it showed when we went climbing. A natural athlete, once she surrendered to trusting her belayer and the equipment, she excelled. She liked climbing, and that made me like her more.

One day we were talking about Yosemite Valley, and I told her all about the place. We looked at schedules to see if we could fit in a trip there before she left. She had a wedding in Boulder in June. We could go to the wedding and then bust out to Yosemite for a week. Perfect right?

We left Gunnison for Boulder in her vehicle on a Thursday afternoon so we could check into the hotel. The employees of the hotel were oh-so fake friendly; I don't know why things like that bother me, but they do. Give me real friendliness or nothing, I say. But when you're throwing down some cash to stay in a place, things like fake friendliness come along with it. Or maybe it's just one of the downsides of Boulder, a place where I usually enjoy myself.

We walked the streets of downtown Boulder, had dinner and drank at a local bar. The next day we ran at the Flatirons, and then checked into yet another hotel for the wedding evening. We ran around town getting nice clothes for the wedding. She dressed me. The only wedding attire I owned was a pink tie that was dumpster dived.

The wedding was a disaster for us. All the other couples were married and kept inquiring about our situation, "Are you moving to the East Coast? Are you getting married soon?"

The event brought out the reality of our situation. We had two more weeks together, and that was it. If I couldn't survive one night as her date for a wedding, there was no way I could survive the long distance Colorado-East Coast relationship. That night in the hotel I told her I didn't think we would be together once she left Colorado. She cried, I felt guilty. It was a sad night in Boulder.

We went to Yosemite anyway. The drive was long, and we tried to talk it out. That first night we stayed in Salt Lake City with a good friend I consider a sister. She'd just broken up with her boyfriend and poured her heart to us over beers and dinner. We didn't bother telling her we'd just broken up. Sometimes there isn't time for everyone to share their feelings.

We arrived in Yosemite and agreed to make the most of the situation. Upon arrival, I learned that the friend I was staying with had just broken up with his girlfriend as well.

She got her first taste of climbing on Yosemite granite, but there was an air of unhappiness between us. We started to argue when left alone. I told her I needed space. It was agreed she would spend a night nearby with a friend from Gunnison who was working for the park service. We would meet up the following day and regroup.

That night after we arrived back at my friend's house, there was a pile of my clothes and belongings in the house, with a note from Lynn saying I needed to call her. When I did, she was in tears. She told me she needed to go home. I stood outside in the meadow in back of the house; the sun was setting. It was the brightest orange I'd ever seen. She asked if I wanted to go back with her. We'd only been in Yosemite for three days, and I'd yet to climb anything serious. I decided to stay. She drove sixteen hours straight back to Gunnison. I was in Yosemite with Scott, a friend who had just broken up with his girlfriend as well. It was a sad situation, but I figured I was where I was supposed to be at that juncture in life, with good company, and a perfect place to reflect on what had just happened.

We'd made plans to climb Stoner's Highway, a ten pitch 5.10 that goes up the center of the Middle Cathedral, right across from the monolith, three thousand foot El Capitan. I figured that it would be just a regular outing on the rock that would pose only minor difficulties given the 5.10 rating, and the fact that I've been climbing at the grade for ten years.

We jokingly dubbed ourselves "Team Breakup" while hiking up the trail to the wall. I was more than eager to do some longer climbing; we'd been festering around the short, one pitch, well travelled climbs for the last few days, and I had the itch to get a few hundred feet off the ground. With a game of rock, paper, scissors, it was decided that I would start out with the leading; an easy, but loose and crumbly pitch led us up to the beginning of the more difficult climbing.

I've always found that when space is gained into the vertical, above the ground, my head space becomes different as well. Reflection is natural when looking around you in the vertical world, and in nature. That day, my thoughts were with Lynn; they were thoughts of guilt. I'd led her all the way out to Yosemite to realize that my own selfishness was at the heart of the journey. I wanted to experience being up high on the walls, and she was a beginner, and we were broken up. How did everything happen so fast?

The meditation and reflection of hanging on the wall is gained through climbing. This day the climbing demanded some serious focus, much more than I had anticipated. After my first mellow lead, it was Scott's turn on the sharp end of the rope. I watched him climb twenty five feet to my left, with no gear off the belay. Had he fallen, he would have violently come swinging back my way. So falling wasn't an option. Scott brilliantly completed the sequence, secured more gear, and then climbed another run-out section. He arrived at the belay, and then I cleaned the pitch, and soon it was my turn for a run out lead.

Scott had set the tone with his incredible, delicate, climbing, and I was determined to emulate his style. I climbed up off the belay about five feet, clipped a piton, a relic from the seventies, all rusted, a 'maybe' piece of protection, as in if you fall maybe it will hold. Then I climbed twenty feet out to the left, heading for a crack system. At this point I was on a small perch, contemplating my fall with the toes of my feet on some good footholds, my hands on some decent holds as well, eyeing the next moves to get to where I could place some pro in a crack that would hold a fall. It's at this point in climbing where complete focus is necessary. I zoned in to the moment, delicately stepped up eyeing a handhold, leaned into it, and stepped up to where I could place some gear. I was safe again, and climbed up a decently protected crack system to the next belay.

Stoner's Highway demanded this type of dangerous, delicate, in the moment type of climbing, pitch after pitch. Scott seemed to get the most difficult pitches, with thirty and even forty foot runouts on 5.10 climbing. He told me he didn't think he could have done the moves if he hadn't just broken up with his girlfriend, and was in the state of mind he was in. I don't think my breakup figured into my risk taking. I just wanted to be up climbing on the wall with a friend, and reflect.

We made it up to the ninth pitch, and it was my turn to lead. The first bolt was a good twenty feet up above the belay, and I couldn't confidently reach it. I climbed back down to Scott, and he went up. He felt the same about the risk, it was too much. We rappelled back to the ground.

I wanted to climb more with Scott, but he was scheduled to go up and climb El Capitan in a couple days and needed to prepare for a four day climb. I was bummed because he was the perfect partner for the situation, but alas, Team Breakup was only destined for one climb.

I spent a few more days in Yosemite Valley, and got my fix, managing to do some multipitch climbing, sorting my thoughts out up on the wall, up above the more complex horizontal world. I arranged a ride back. Tory, one of my best friends, was moving back to Gunnison after three years in Los Angeles. He welcomed the company, and he also listened to me talk about Lynn. A good listener, who is also a good friend, is invaluable. He told me about his struggles with women and relationships, too. All of our struggles as humans are similar.

Back in Gunnison, Lynn was set to leave in a week. I met up with her for coffee the morning I returned from California. She shared with me just how upset she truly was about my selfishness in Yosemite. I felt sad. I tried my best to listen and not be defensive. In relationships, I don't know if it's better to be heartbroken or the heartbreaker.

A week passed, and we didn't see each other. Finally it was her last night in town. We had a few items of each other's and agreed to exchange them at her house, and say goodbye. It was raining when I rode my bike over there. Her dog was the first thing I saw on the porch. A dog that had been previously abused, she was confused by all the boxes packed up. It was sad. Moving is a confusing thing.

We said goodbye and wished each other well. As we hugged, I looked over her shoulder to see a pile of new climbing gear. Since we'd parted in Yosemite two weeks ago, she'd purchased a rope and more equipment. She had the bug. At least I gave her something, I thought, the love for climbing.

It's been a couple months now. It's fall again. We exchange emails about our lives, she's found places to climb in the east, and she's leading now. Again, I feel confident about life, and optimistic. I've finally experienced being in love. It only took thirty one years. Once you've loved, life is different. For all of my dating life, I wondered if I would ever truly love and feel confident enough to share that; now I know that's possible.

As I finish this, my life is in boxes, preparing for a move, down south to Durango, a warmer Colorado mountain town. We climbers, more often than not, live transient lifestyles. We know that life is temporary, change is the only constant. What is there to hold onto, to believe in?

One truth for me still stands out; something a wise climber friend said to me, "Women are the greatest thing on this planet."

Well, women and climbing, of course.

19 MARY JANE, A CLIMBER'S THOUGHTS ON THE LEGALIZATION OF MARIJUANA

El Portrero Chico in Hidalgo, Mexico, is where we go to rock climb. It was New Year's Eve, and we were there to escape the Colorado cold. The limestone walls soar into the heavens; tilt your head back to see vertical walls full of vegetation, walls where even palm trees grow out of the rock.

We are athletes, but we like to party. Even the best of the best rock climbers, the Spiderman types who dangle a thousand feet above the ground on vertical terrain without a rope, partake. Why is marijuana so popular with climbers? Perhaps it is that while climbing is an intense activity demanding focus and concentration, weed provides just the opposite experience.

We were on the hunt for some weed, *mota*, ganja, herb, whatever you'd like to call it, for a few days. Some years it's easy to find; this year it was not. The word from fellow climbers is to not even bother trying. Gangsters control all the marijuana distribution.

Thousands have died in the drug war in the last few years in Mexico. Much of this death can be linked to the drug consumption in the United States. Even in Mexico, we don't see it; we just hear about it. Hidalgo is a safe haven, a small town, where all the locals smile and wave.

This year we finally made friends with some locals from the nearby *cuidad* of Monterrey, the second largest city of Mexico. They are sweet, exotic and naturally open. They tell us about their culture, about the *federales,* who can and will harass anyone and everyone, for no reason.

In the United States, many of us have grudges against the police, but where we live in Colorado, the cops do mostly protect and serve. In Mexico, every person has the potential to be harassed by the

117

federales. It was our *amigas* that eventually scored us weed, at a big climbing party on New Year's Eve. It's terrible, the type that high school kids smoke: brick weed that is brown and old.

If there is one experience in my life that has taught me patience, it's the border crossing after the holidays. It seemed like the entire country of Mexico was going back to the United States after Christmas and New Year's. We waited in traffic for hours, staring out the windows to the desolate landscape, to the vendors that sell statues of Jesus and the Virgin Mary, and *elote*, a version of corn on the cob with pepper spices and mayonnaise. People in wheelchairs, without arms or strange tumors on their faces begging for money, shacks next to the highway that make you sad, trash everywhere. We hear a lot of casual racism against Mexicans in the United States, especially the ones that don't know good English and perform minimum wage jobs. How could we ever hate someone for doing a shitty job for little money? After a week in Mexico, I don't blame them for coming up to *Estados Unidos*.

After five hours to cover less than five miles, we arrived at the border. A Subaru from Colorado must be suspicious, because our car was picked as one the border patrol would like to search. We're prepared for a time consuming process of the cops going through all our possessions, looking at our climbing chalk and thinking it's a drug or something, but times have changed, an infrared machine attached to a van scans over the Subaru in two minutes, and we are cleared to go. Freedom!

A couple more border checkpoints make me wonder how drugs ever make it into our country from Mexico. It's hard to believe that the drug trade is a multi-million dollar economy, one that is tearing Mexico apart to feed the American appetite for a change of mood and perspective.

I'd been hearing talk and reading the daily, front page, features in the *Denver Post*. Medical marijuana is a booming business in Colorado.

There are over a hundred dispensaries in Denver alone. Security companies have been getting more work from the related boom, and so have insurance companies and lawyers. A few cannabis colleges have opened up, offering seminars on everything from opening up a dispensary to cooking classes to presentations on marijuana laws. It's been said that medical marijuana has been the only booming business in Colorado during our current recession.

The fiscal impact is interesting, patients are getting the medicine they need and a culture that has operated underground and illegally for so long is now on every block in the great city of Denver. Pot dealers used to be considered drug dealers. Now with the blink of an eye, marijuana can be purchased legally at hundreds of different shops.

There I sat with my good friend Jack in a friendly neighborhood dispensary, Colfax Wellness Center. All of the pot shops have goofy names like this: Alternative Healing, A Mile High, Sweet Leaf Compassion, The Kind Room, etc. In the waiting room, we sat patiently but eager for our turn to get a look at the pot. Next to me was an old man, who appeared as though his medical marijuana use was actually legit. His hands were shaking, but he must've been medicated because the guy was grinning from ear to ear saying how relieved he was that weed was finally legal, so that he didn't have to worry about it anymore.

This was Jack's first visit to a dispensary. He'd just obtained his card from a doctor in the same facility granting him the necessary paperwork, notarized and all, to purchase marijuana legally. His condition was pain from a separated shoulder. I'd begun my ventures into legal weed a couple weeks ago after receiving my medical marijuana card. My condition was pain from tendonitis.

While we waited, a gentleman who had some sort of important role with the dispensary gave us a tour of the facility, which included his opinion on all things weed. He showed us all the different kinds of edibles: suckers, ice cream, brownies and cheesecake, all the sugar products one could imagine with weed in them. He showed us the grow room. In the past, a grow room was an exclusive thing that the grower would only show the most trusted of friends. Growing operations have put thousands of Americans in jail in the past, and still do in places where marijuana is illegal.

The plant itself is magnetic and energetic, the brightest of greens. The grow room displayed the lights necessary to grow high quality indoor herb, and there were plants at different stages in the process. If we wanted plants, clones were available for purchase. As a medical marijuana cardholder, I can legally grow some plants myself. I can also have a caregiver grow for me as well.

After a lengthy wait, we were able to see the man with the weed. He looked like a guy who had already been smoking weed before coming to work, but I guess when your job is to sell weed, legally for a living, you are just sampling the product.

We sat opposite of him at his desk. On the desk were twenty different kinds of weed in jars with various names: Trainwreck, Skunk, Purple Haze, Ice O Later, Afghanny, Sage, etc.

In between yawns, the slightly overweight, lackadaisical middle aged man went into great detail on the kinds of pot, and the effect that each would have on the user. The Afghanny-Trainwreck, an indica, would get you wasted. His customers used that and gave him feedback, and they were attached to the couch after using it. Others, like the Sage, were sativa, so the effect would be energizing and stimulating, something he said one would use if she were about to rake the leaves. He went on and on; we just wanted to get on with our day. He had us cornered though, we were in his office, and we were locked into purchasing something. It felt like we were locked into a poker game. I bought some of his special suckers. Jack bought some weed, and after a half an hour of this infomercial like experience, we were on our way.

Many jobs have been created by legalizing and legitimizing medical marijuana. Or maybe it should be said those illegal jobs have become legal. It's been a boost to the Colorado economy, creating jobs, serving medicine to those who need it and keeping people who partake and are involved in the industry out of trouble with the law.

How this will affect our neighbors, our brothers and sisters to the south in Mexico, is yet to be seen. If marijuana was legal in the U.S. and Mexico, would it no longer be controlled by gangs and *federales*? Would that then quiet the drug war in Mexico? Would fewer people be killed? Could marijuana be a viable, legal cash crop in Mexico?

Now that I'm done with this piece, I can let my mind go. I take a legal hit, and think of all those that obtain their weed illegally through the gangsters, through the illegal, corrupt Mexican drug trade, one that has claimed thousands and thousands of lives, and wonder if the trend towards legalization will continue?

20 TRYING TO HANG WITH BEN JOHNSON

When I run with Ben Johnson, I know he's always going to be gone, like Forrest Gump running across that football field in Alabama. He was a state champion high school runner, two-time winner of the local 2.6 mile sprint up W Mountain in Gunnison, Colorado, and probably has a list of victories I don't even know about.

When I'm road biking with Ben, I use a trick that ensures I can keep up with him. If I let him stay in the lead, I can simply stay right behind him and draft, which basically means he does all the work, and I can reap the benefits and use gravity to my advantage. This ensures that I stay with him while riding and also enables me to save energy.

One weekend, mid-November high in the Rockies, I had the good fortune to bike with Ben one day and run with him the next. Well it wasn't just us, our good friend Al Smith III, a badass in his own right, was along for both adventures as well.

With outdoor adventures, I typically both love and hate Ben, with the hate always being a short term emotion because Ben typically pushes me past my perceived limits, and the love always lasting.

I think I was probably hating Ben Saturday afternoon when we were road biking up Taylor Canyon, with an hour of sunlight left, on icy roads on skinny tires and my fingers were so cold they were going numb. This was a leisurely workout for Ben, a forty mile afternoon ride in winter like conditions. When I was freezing and complaining, he even offered up his warm pair of gloves and an extra jacket, which I gladly accepted.

Things really got epic as we rounded Almont, ten miles out from Gunnison, and Al got his second flat of the day. We didn't have an extra tube between the three of us, so like any good Coloradoan, Al stuck his thumb out and hitched a ride back to town. Four miles to go, there was barely any daylight as I looked over to see a buck running parallel to our bikes. The deer hopped with us as we rode till he made a dramatic dash across the road and then jumped over a fence to safety in a rancher's field.

With the sun setting and still two miles to go, Ben turned on a light on the back of his bike so that the passing vehicles would see us; at the same time the darkness fell and it began to snow. I suffered through this as my feet froze up and felt like ice blocks.

When I finally arrived home, I could barely waddle up the flight of stairs to my house. I sat inside with a nice adrenaline rush, and felt incredibly alive. (Then I spent the next half an hour warming my feet up.) If I didn't have Ben Johnson in my life I probably would have stayed inside and been lazy that cold mid-November afternoon in The Rockies.

The next day we were headed to the Orvis Hot Springs to soak and recover from the ride. Ben suggested to me and Al that we should, "go for a little run before soaking." We agreed, and I pictured running for a little while around the town of Ouray.

Ben took us past the Box Canyon in Ouray up to a dirt road and then drove back for a few miles. He parked his car, and I looked up the road. It was a steep hill, covered mostly in snow. Al remarked how steep it was and that it would be a shock to the system to start the run with such a dramatic incline. Ben shrugged it off, making a masculine comment and just started running up. I tried to hang with him for about five minutes, and then soon Al and I quickly lost him as he ran into the hills.

Al and I power walked some of the sections and a couple miles into it the road became a small cross-country ski trail in a foot and a half of snow. Two hundred foot ice falls to the left on four hundred foot rock walls. Ice climbers dangled off an overhang to the right. We couldn't see him, but we knew Ben was still running.

We headed back, running and walking for the hour time slot that we agreed upon. After an hour, we knew Ben wouldn't be back exactly on time, but ten minutes after the hour had passed he was there.

"Good workout," he said in his Colorado way of talking.

Yes it was Ben. It always is with you.

Originally published in the Crested Butte Weekly (RIP) in the winter of 2009-10.

21 THE BLACK CANYON

I thought we couldn't do it
But we did
I thought the end
Was upon us, but it wasn't
Doomsday ended up being a
Rebirth.
I can't understand exactly how we did it

But we did, the good guys won
A victory against evil, a real evil
The evil that is doubt

And I meant it when I said reborn
I feel reborn

I feel as young as the blue in the sky
You taught me that positivity would be
The only way to survive,
And you were right
That face first with a smile
Was the only way to face my
Fear
That the negative mind would only connect
With negativity

But the mind that doesn't think negatively
Would connect on a whole other level
The level of rocks, trees, birds
And souls fighting
Fighting for freedom, wildness and perseverance

The canyon let us test these philosophies
A God from this peaceful paradise gave us answers
A few, the most important ones came from within
And the philosophies held true
And we found that love isn't so far away
The love for yourself and what you are capable of

It all lies within
The love for your brothers and sisters
The mountains and rivers
Crazy, crazy experience

*A version of this poem was originally published in the Gunnison Valley Journal,
fourth edition.*

22 ZEN DISHWASHING

"I got 99 problems but a dish ain't one."

Washing dishes was my first real job at the ripe age of sixteen. Today, at twice that age, it is still my occupation. What lies in the space of those sixteen years is the Zen of dishwashing.

I'd be willing to bet half the people living in Crested Butte have been a dish diver at one time or another. Our economy demands that most of us take jobs we are overqualified to do. Something that the economy in the Gunnison Valley also demands is creativity, so I suppose it is fitting that Zen dishwashing was born in Crested Butte. Former dishwasher, Garth Mangels of Crested Butte, gets credit for coining the term.

Dishwashing was my main occupation during my collegiate years, and I met a ton of characters working in the restaurants of the Valley. One of the most memorable characters is the first Zen dishwasher I ever met, Tim Foulkes.

I'd been diving in the dish pit at The Palace in Gunnison for a couple of months, and was ready to move up to cooking. I was twenty and ambitious; the dishwasher was the lowliest place in the restaurant, and I was tired of being the last person in the joint when the place closed down. The cooks would promptly start drinking at the bar when their shift was over, leaving me to finish up on my own.

Plus, I'd nearly died in that dish pit, when I unknowingly turned on the disposal one day with a big sharp knife in it, and it came flying out, blade first, barely missing me. It would have been a tragic death for a young diver.

Tim loved death metal, and the main benefit of The Palace was that the diver had his own stereo, a key element attaining Zen in the dish pit. Back then, I was somewhat of a Deadhead, which could have put us at odds with each other, but luckily it didn't.

I'd never seen a diver as content as Tim in the pit. He would simply blast his death metal and get into the zone. Since I'd recently been in his shoes, I'd stay a bit later, helping him put the dishes away so he wasn't alone finishing up while everyone else partied at the bar.

Another thing about Tim was that he refused to advance to cooking. I'd never seen someone do that, and couldn't conceive why one would hold on to an occupation that paid less, and was treated worse. But visionaries are often doubted at first.

This place, in those days, was a little too casual about the drinking; the boss was a so-called recovering alcoholic who still drank. Anyways, the place wasn't turning a profit, and closed down after I'd only worked with Tim for a few months.

I followed Tim to the Green Lizard, a Mexican joint, with alcoholic managers, and the worst dish pit I've ever seen. No machine, just a sink, and lots of oils from all the fried food. The only ray of light and fresh air was a small vent right in front of my face. That space was even violated one day when a cook pulled a prank on me, blowing flour through it, covering my face in white powder.

Fortunately, the unhappy, alcoholic managers would not stick around in the evening, and we'd be left alone. Not all of the cooks were mean, some were climbing buddies of mine, and we'd take safety meetings near the pit, blowing the marijuana smoke into the vents above the grills. A couple of times police officers would come in for food, just after the meetings, but the smell was masked by the fryers and other food on the stovetops.

I jumped at the chance to advance to cooking, leaving behind the cramped dish pit, but moving closer to working with the annoying, alcoholic manager. He always gave me and everyone else a hard time. So it was only a matter of time before I got sick of this job, and one summer day I called in and told them I was done.

I tried to seek employment with my friend Rich Lombardo, who owned the now gone Mexican joint Serranos, in Gunnison, but he didn't need any help. So he called up to some restaurant owners in Crested Butte, and set me up with an interview at Donita's Cantina.

The start of my diving career at Donita's was unremarkable. I showed up, washed some dishes, went home and repeated. There wasn't much of a social scene for me; no climbers worked there, and I didn't have any friends that worked there either. But it was a job, and it paid more than the places in Gunnison, so I continued on.

During this time period of my life, I started to experiment with minimizing bills and maximizing recreation time. I was studying Recreation in college, and I figured it was time to take a semester off for some field research. My lease ran up at the same time, and I put my domestic belongings in a storage area and moved into a tent.

It was a glorious period, with plenty of time for climbing and camping, and virtually no living expenses, save for gasoline, gear and food. I wrote poetry by the fire when I camped alone, and spent a lot of time inside my head just thinking.

I finally graduated, and realized that there were warmer places than the Gunnison Valley to camp out and be a climbing bum/dishwasher. So, the first winter after graduating, I packed up and traveled to Joshua Tree in southern California. I scored a job at a restaurant called Crossroads. I walked in and told the manager that I was the best dishwasher in Colorado. It must have worked because I found myself employed in their modest, three sink, dishwashing station the next day.

It was a winter of a hundred days of camping, naked dance parties atop rock formations, plenty of climbing, and lots of free food from Crossroads. The two head cooks could not have been more different from each other: one was a hard working, thirty something woman who cursed up a storm, and the other was a beautiful, quiet Asian woman, a climber, who graduated from Yale. I made friends with both, as well as the other two cooks, who were eager to try climbing. I took them climbing, and in turn they treated me with a high level of respect, something that is often hard to come by as a new dishwasher in a kitchen.

It was as simple as my life had ever been. Moments of contentment came and went, and I pondered how long this simple life of climbing, camping and washing dishes could be satisfying.

By April, Joshua Tree started to heat up, and all signs pointed that I should return back to Colorado. So I went back to Donita's. The dish pit seemed bigger and cleaner than ever after working in a cramped space without a dish machine.

One cook at Donita's, however, was always messing with my Zen. He would shout obscenities at me, and rudely place dishes in my area by basically throwing them at me. He also dissed my music. By now, my music of choice was hip-hop, as I'd become less of a hippie. One day I put some Outkast on, and he started complaining about it, running off a slew of obscenities. It was either time to punch him in the face, or walk out. I chose the latter. The same cook also had a plate thrown at him by another dishwasher whom he was disrespecting. I wish I could have seen that.

A couple of years ago, I thought I had an opportunity to get out of the dishwashing game forever. I was working for minimum wage, washing dishes in Salt Lake City, when I got a call from my alma mater. The college's Office of Public Relations and Communications was looking for a writer. I jumped at the chance, and I was quickly promoted to full time. I thought my days of diving were behind me.

I went almost two solid years without commercially washing a dish. However, with the downfall in the economy, my job was cut to half time, and I inquired up at Donita's. They took me back in.

Things were better now in the kitchen. The stars had aligned for some Zen dishwashing to take place. The cooks were friendly; I was being treated with respect; the music was generally good and safety meetings were tolerated.

But now, the problem was with me. I wasn't content in the dish pit. I thought about it long and hard. What had changed? Had I learned all the lessons in life that the dish pit had to teach me?

I reached out to fellow writers and philosophers to figure out where I went wrong. One friend, Nathan Kubes, an artist from Gunnison, wrote back to me, "The term the Zen of dishwashing is right on. This drudgery is a serious pain in the arse, it wounds our ego, it exhausts our bodies, tires our minds, and it seriously inhibits inspiration."

What did I know about Zen? I realized I knew very little. Could suffering with the dishes teach me as much as when I was content with the job? Was I really after Zen dishwashing or was I searching for something else?

I sought more information from Nathan and wrote to him to see if he had any readings he recommended on Zen. He wrote back, "You want to read about Zen? Read the phone book."

A clever answer, his thoughts had served their purpose. I began to look at diving with a new perspective. Meditation or Zen are not things that are easily attained; nor is finding happiness while holding down a mediocre job that you are beyond qualified to do. The whole summer I'd been learning more lessons about the Zen of dishwashing, and I thought I had lost the path. I was on it more than ever.

The busy summer has passed. While many are sad to see the summer go, in Crested Butte we, overqualified, grunt workers welcome the autumn, or the off season with joy, especially if we've saved money and can recreate during the time when tourists are not recreating here.

I realize after this most recent season of diving, my return to the ol' dish pit, after a long hiatus, that I don't need to continue to look for Zen dishwashing; it's always there. There's Zen in every moment, learning opportunities in every situation, good or bad.

What I am searching for now is the dishwasher's nirvana, and I'm going to be thinking about that in the next couple of months while I'm enjoying the fruits of my labor, time off, recreating in the wild lands of the west.

A version of this story was originally published in the Crested Butte Magazine, Summer 2011.

23 THE FREEDOM MOBILE

Our vehicles make statements about our lifestyles, and in the mountain town of Crested Butte, Colorado there is quite the diversity in modes of transportation. From the high class Hummer SUVs to the old Subaru station wagon that checks in well over 200,000 miles, the car we drive can be a dead giveaway to the activities we pursue. I often wonder what strangers think of my car, an old 1988 Mazda that is spray painted red, white and blue, most commonly known as The Freedom Mobile.

Ever since I saw the classic 1969 American road movie *Easy Rider* with Peter Fonda and Jack Nicholson, I've wanted to paint a vehicle in the colors of our country. I've always sensed that us mountain folk are living out our own version of the American Dream up here in the Gunnison Valley, and my car is representative of our unique culture. Adding to the mystique, I also wanted to feature the OM symbol, to show that the east and west can come together. To represent that I am a proud American, who has also been heavily influenced by the ancient, Indian based art of yoga.

Reactions to The Freedom Mobile have been mostly positive since I graffiti-ed it up with my friend and artist, Nathan Kubes, three years ago. I can count on children smiling and pointing at it, supportive nods from people on townies crossing Elk Ave., and my fellow climbers saying, "I love your car" at various locales across the west. The most predictable response, however, is from hitchhikers, as I slow down to pull over. Their response, with a glimmer of hope in their eyes, is something to the effect of, "I knew you were going to pick me up."

I'm proud to drive a vehicle that elicits such a response. It took some time to get to this level of pride, though. The very next day after we first painted the car, I was pulled over by the police, saying something about my headlights not working properly. I thought they were, and wondered if I'd just set myself up for getting pulled over all the time. It took some time getting used to driving a car that attracted such attention.

A couple months later, I had a first date, at the Almont bar of all places. (The woman was living in Crested Butte, and I was living in Gunnison; a good midway meeting point I thought.) I had the usual butterflies of a first date, and as I walked out to get in my car for the drive, I wished to the heavens that I hadn't painted my car in such an outlandish manner, so I could just present myself in somewhat of a normal way. She ended up loving The Freedom Mobile though, and I learned an important lesson that our inner freak is usually a beautiful thing, and we should not hide it; if someone is a kindred spirit they'll love what is inside you.

Something I did in the Freedom Mobile, that I never dreamed would happen, was taking it on a major rock climbing road trip, across the Western United States. It all went down like this. I'd just lost my full time with benefits job in Gunnison, with the downturn in the economy, and recently broken up with the first woman I'd ever been in love with. I needed to get out of the valley, and I'd made plans to move down south, to Durango for a fresh start. In the interim, my friend Dave and I would take a month long road trip. It would be one of those coming of age trips to do something exciting, and forget about the trials and tribulations of the past.

At the last minute, Dave's truck broke down, and now the trip relied on The Freedom Mobile. With nothing to lose, I decided to take Freedom on the trip. We drove to Red Rocks in Las Vegas, Nevada down to Joshua Tree, California, up to Yosemite, to Vegas again, and finally down to Durango. There were many moments of pure bliss, and the country's reception of The Freedom Mobile was incredible. At one moment, driving in southern Utah, a woman sitting shotgun in an old truck, with oxygen hooked up to her nose, pulled up next to us, and gave the biggest grin I'd ever seen, and two thumbs up. Later that same day, pulling into a gas station in the Middle of Nowhere, Utah, some good ol' boy mechanics were staring us down. We were slightly defensive until they started talking, "Nice car, it looks like something Evil Knievel would drive."

Durango ended up embracing The Freedom Mobile, and there are more spray painted cars there per capita than any other place in Colorado I've been. Work ended up being scarce in Durango, as it is many places in our country these days, and when the spring ended, I found myself returning to Crested Butte for the summer.

The Freedom Mobile made its first appearance in Crested Butte's Fourth of July parade, and somehow I managed to convince sixteen of my closest friends to spell out The Freedom Mobile in body paint across their stomachs and chests. The wildest incident, though, came later, in the fall, as the deadline for this piece was approaching.

I'd teamed up my friend, Braden Gunem, to do a photo shoot for this article. He rigged up a camera on the front of my car, with all sorts of lighting inside; including a small rag in a bottle he wanted to light on fire to add a wild touch to the photos. While we were keeping our eyes peeled for the police, I looked up to the last rays of daylight to see a major townie takeover headed our way. I couldn't believe my eyes. It was the Brick Oven Pizzeria's softball team, dressed complete with their signature red, yellow and green tank tops, and hairnets on their townies; thirty of them, followed by a police officer.

As we watched it all go down, wondering what was going to happen, the police officer ended up escorting the Rasta Hairnet townie takeover down Elk Ave. Only in Crested Butte! With the police busy escorting the wild Brick Oven crew, we commenced with our unorthodox photo shoot. The result is the cover shot for this book.

I never know what's around the corner for The Freedom Mobile, and I like it like that. It's headed back down to Durango for the winter, so it won't be rolling the streets of Crested Butte when the snow falls. The spirit of Crested Butte lives in The Freedom Mobile, wherever it may go though. Let freedom ring!

A version of this piece was originally published in the Crested Butte Magazine, Winter 2011-12.

24 LAST THOUGHTS ON ADAM LAWTON

Adam Lawton has been in my thoughts for all my waking hours since he was killed in an avalanche on January 6th, 2012, in British Columbia. I've wanted to write about him since it happened, but I've been unable to. There is a time and place to write, just like Allen Ginsberg once said, "I won't write my poem till I'm in my right mind."

Those of you who knew Adam are feeling his departure in one way or another. He was a great man and a great friend, the type of individual I wish there were more of in this sometimes harsh world. He was a light. He was a leader. He encouraged thinking and questioning, but never spent so much time doing those things that he annoyed or did not live to the utmost extent. He loved skiing, running, biking, climbing and floating down rivers. He loved women. He loved good food. He loved yoga. He loved life and shared that love so much that it grew exponentially in all our hearts, and will continue to grow.

I first met Adam at Western State College in 2000, and we'd been paired up to deliver a presentation on Leave No Trace for a Recreation class. I couldn't even begin to recall the specifics of what we discussed during our meeting in the College Union, but I do remember that he possessed a lust for living, and a hunger to learn more about the world and pursue that knowledge in an experiential way. I got a feeling that we were both in college, in Gunnison, not simply to get a degree for a certain amount of knowledge of a career path, but to access higher learning in the great outdoors, with a community of people that shared this hunger for living life to the fullest.

Over the years, Adam and I grew closer, and in a roundabout way, we ended up sharing all the same friends in the Gunnison Valley. Like minded people have a way of finding one another. I remember one day in Crested Butte, he was describing his life, "I feel like every day is the best day of my life. I thought yesterday was the best day of my life, and then today was the best day of my life." It was just the opposite of the scene in *Office Space* where the main character is describing every day as being the worst day of his life. The mountains were Adam's rightful home, and he was happy in the mountains.

Eventually, Adam moved to Salt Lake City, Utah, to pursue an even higher education, at a graduate program at the University of Utah, and the powder of the nearby Wasatch Mountains. I remember him quoting another skier, "The license plates don't lie," talking about the slogan written on the Utah plates, Greatest Snow on Earth.

I passed through Salt Lake City in my post collegiate wanderings of the west more than once, and Adam was a most hospitable host. He always had various new friends and new stories to tell. One year, while passing through Salt Lake, I ended up running out of money there, and had to get a job. His hospitality never wavered and he let me crash on his couch as often as needed.

He loved skiing so much, I am in awe of how he excelled at climbing, biking, running and river activities. Last I talked to him, he was excited about the idea of long, ultra running races. He always seemed to remain passionate about skiing, while also doing something new, and he always wanted to share that passion.

Adam was interested in so many things, and now, in retrospect, I wish I'd taken notes about our conversations. He had an open mind, the true definition of an open mind, maybe so much that his mind was continually expanding. He was certainly into mind expansion. His heart was ever expanding as well, and I think the greatest advice he ever told me was to breathe.

We're all grieving over you, Adam, and I felt the huge loss of your departure in the weeping of all our shared friends as the news broke that you'd been killed in an avalanche. Everyone is dealing with it differently; people deal with death in different ways. In some way, we'll never be the same without you. We are better for having known you. The world is a better place because you lived. We hope to see you again, and your spirit is always with us. I can feel it right now as these tears spill onto my keyboard.

25 INDIAN CREEK REFLECTION

The good times are moving fast these days, zipping by as we fly through space on this big ball of rock. As a writer, it is my job to record, to pause, to go back in time, if only slightly, and squeeze the juice out of divine moments, and produce something special for those that read.

I once had a Recreation professor in college say our moments in the outdoors have less meaning if we don't reflect upon them afterwards. I think it's technically called a debrief. I find truth in that idea as I sit here and write now, recharging and reenergizing for the next climbing excursion.

The red rock desert of Indian Creek canyon is my home. I would not be opposed to have my ashes scattered there after my time here is done. I cannot fathom death now, being so alive, yet someday it will come. I just hope I can grow old, write, climb, and love more than I already have. I've got plans and dreams.

This place, a seemingly endless corridor of red rock walls and towers with perfect cracks, little trace of man's impacts, desert trees and bushes, free camping in the truest sense of the word, birds, lizards, bunny rabbits, and deer; it is a life changing place. Personally, it consumes me, and living in Durango, Colorado just two and a half hours away, well it's a part of my existence, and it gives and takes energy to be a part of it.

I've been learning lately to give one hundred percent into life; today is the only day we are truly given. Yesterday is dead. Tomorrow is a dream. So at Indian Creek, I throw myself at the cracks: finger, off-finger, hand, wide hands, off-width, chimney; the fissures created by time and pressure are the objects of a climber's desire. They are also known as the most perfect cracks in the world. And they are in my backyard. Perhaps I would have achieved more in life if I were not distracted by this pursuit, or maybe the opposite. Maybe these cracks inspire me to strive for perfection, as perfect as they are. Or maybe it is my friends, my climbing partners that inspire.

Those cracks, there are thousands and thousands in the red rock desert, in the heart of Utah. Only a few can be seen from the road, those are usually the large ones, the ones that swallow our bodies, the off-widths that actually seem to be in fashion right now in climbing. We have to hike to the cracks, and then we cannot resist climbing them. The most perfect are sought out first, those that stretch for a hundred feet or more, the ones that fit our hands and fingers perfectly are the best. The sensation is foreign at first. Watch a first time Indian Creek climber try to climb a crack. It is a ridiculous struggle, as the crowd below instructs how to insert a climbing shoe into a crack, then the hand or fingers. Usually hands are the best appendages to insert into a fissure. Then watch an experienced Indian Creek climber, on a climb that is well within their ability level. They look like they don't need the rope, or the camming units they stuff into the crack and clip the rope to. It looks intuitive, like vertical hiking.

We all must find challenges, though, in climbing, and continually reach out of our comfort zones, to grow. There isn't a climber on this earth that couldn't find a challenge at Indian Creek. Climbers are all equal, or at least we should be. The struggle is where we unite. We get out what we put in.

I am obsessed with this pursuit, and luckily, I have a lot of friends that are into it too, some as obsessed as me, some even much more so. I know I'll have people to share this passion with until I am old and gray. It's strange to still have this comfort, as I am close to being in my mid-thirties. I once thought this was a pursuit for my youth, now I know it is a lifelong pursuit, and that is a good thing. The longer I live, the more climbs I learn about that I want to try. .

Try hard. That's an important thing in climbing. Last weekend I tried so hard it hurt. I tried so hard I couldn't try anymore, until the cracks above were painful just to look at. Just before that, in the climbing bliss, an evening sunset, my muscles feeling a nice pump, with just enough water in the body, I turned to my friend Lindsey, and asked why we ever leave this place. It felt like heaven, a utopia. The sun gave a red ray on an adjacent sandstone wall, as if this weren't even real. The Bridger Jack towers stood proudly, staggering monuments to present and future climbing, each one its own formation, some higher than others, some more slender at the top, one looking like just a little capstone on a brilliant four hundred foot monument of maroon sandstone. The air cool, it was just too hot earlier, but now it has cooled, nothing lasts forever, not even that perfect moment. Especially the perfect moments, they fly by as quick as a bird zips by us on a cliff. The valley floor, greening up, any direction in that valley would lead to more sandstone walls, a maze of delight and adventure for a rock climber.

The next day, I knew why we leave. We returned to my favorite crack climbing cliff in the world, Broken Tooth, on a mission for one last climb. Hiking up the well built trail from volunteers, rock steps, and twists and turns built by minds that understood trails, my body didn't seem to want to do it anymore. My legs and muscles burned. The rock wall in front grew closer. I was relieved.

The mission was to retrieve a couple cams a friend had to bail on the day before. It was our fourth day of climbing at Indian Creek. Day one and two a climber may feel indestructible, day four is different. Day four, as my friend Al says, "The spirit was willing, but the body was spongy and weak."

The day before, another friend had climbed a sucker crack adjacent of the prime line that was supposed to be climbed, a crack with no anchors, and one where the rock quality goes from perfect to suspect; I climbed up to the cams, and then down aided, praying other cams would not blow out of the rock, or become stuck. I'd been suckered into this crack before, and felt obligated to retrieve our friend's gear. I then climbed up the correct line, setting up a top rope for Al, who belayed me. Lowering off, the rock was heating up, the darker rock hot to touch, and I was growing woozy, light headed, weak, ready to return home.

And then I realized why we leave. It is a home, but just one home; the climber has more than one home. It's as simple as that. As simple as needing a shower, and rest. To recover.

It would be interesting if the human body never tired. If we could go on for days and days climbing at our limits, if we could live for hundreds of years, instead of a maximum of just under a hundred, but we don't, at least not yet. We're living in a world of infinite possibilities, with a finite amount of time.

When it all comes down to it, I only enjoy my active time when I've given one hundred percent, when I have tried hard. Same thing with my down time, if there is that itch, that energy to do something, I won't enjoy just sitting there, unless I am in meditation or yoga, but that is another essay.

As for now, I've learned something in reflection, in repose, I'm still dreaming about Indian Creek. I always will be. It is a part of me, a part of the land I live within. I love it. I love the climbing partners that love it, too. We love the pain and the glory. We love the crack. It is a painful, fiendish, obsessive love affair.

My body is not ready to return just yet. There is more rest that is needed. More yoga that must be done. More water that I must drink and food to eat. Across my room where I write and rest, my cams and ropes and other climbing gear sit there, just waiting to be used on the rock, just as my body, when it has recovered, will be willing to be thrown upon those cracks, those rocks, in search of something.

THANKS AND ACKNOWLEDGMENTS

I love writing, and the journey towards becoming a professional has been long and difficult. It's one that has made me realize that failure is an essential ingredient to the learning process. Fortunately, I've been blessed to have teachers and editors in my life that inspired me to endure on the writing path.

George Sibley was the faculty advisor when I wrote for the student newspaper, *Top O' the World* at Western State College of Colorado. He gave me encouragement in abundance, as I struggled to create the marriage between passion and professionalism in my writing.

Chris Dickey, publisher of the *Gunnison Country Times*, the first publication that ever paid me to write anything. Chris stayed patient with me as I learned the craft, and never said no to a good story idea. He is the quintessential small town newspaper man.

Sandy Fails, editor of *Crested Butte Magazine*, has published my stories of climbing and mountain town culture. While many mountain towns have these free, glossy magazines that represent the areas, none are as fine or genuine as the *Crested Butte Magazine*.

Alison Osius, executive editor of *Rock and Ice* magazine, worked with me to get my first stories published in a major magazine, and has always pushed me to think about every word and sentence.

Katherine Ives, editor in chief at the *Alpinist*, has spent time with a couple of my pieces, and although I've yet to publish anything with the *Alpinist*, her insights and critique have been greatly appreciated.

Mike Rosso, editor and publisher of *Colorado Central Magazine*, a fine regional magazine based out of Salida, Colorado that I've written several articles for. Mike clearly loves the region that *Colorado Central Magazine* covers, and his magazine shows that.

John Fayhee, editor of the *Mountain Gazette*, for your work with some of my earlier pieces. Your advice towards becoming a professional has been invaluable, and all of us readers appreciate your labor of love to keep the *Mountain Gazette* alive and interesting.

Tyler Sage, a professor of English, who I took two Extended Studies courses with at Western State College of Colorado, after I was already a so-called professional. Tyler taught his classes in an open, workshop style format, and brought everyone together, in a positive way to analyze pieces of writing. Several of the stories in this book were improved because of those sessions.

Tracey Koehler, my supervisor during my years working in the Office of Public Relations and Communications at Western State College of Colorado, has read and edited more of my work than anyone else. Tracey was a blessing for my writing more than she probably knows.

Jessica Schocker, my first true love, who I can always count on to look at my work, even while she is busy with a million other things. You taught me to believe in love, and believe in myself.

Will Sands and Missy Vogel at the *Durango Telegraph*, my latest freelance newspaper gig. I was looking for a reason to move to Durango, and Will helped seal the deal by telling me I could freelance for their paper. Missy, I look forward to writing for the paper with you at the helm, as well as more fun with the "Ask the Diver" column.

Will Gray, former editor at *National Geographic*, and professor of English at San Juan College. Through his creative writing course in the Continuing Education program at Fort Lewis College, in Durango, Colorado, I learned an immense amount about the craft of writing. I hope to study more with Will in the future.

My climbing partners are also essential to any and every success

I've ever had, and to you I owe my life and my work. I'd like to acknowledge my long term climbing partners and mentors: Tim Stypolkowsi, Tim Foulkes, Dave Ahrens, Shaun Matusewicz, Phillip Street, Mark Grundon, Scott Borden, Dave Marcinowski, Ben Johnson, Torrance Maurer, Leo Malloy, Brent Armstrong, Sara Smith, Keith Brett, Shane Neidert, Chris Kovac, Matt Willis, Jerid Lewton, Dane Molinaro, Adam Ferro, Jonathan Schaffer, Lindsey Schauer, Seth Calkins, Todd Glew, Matt Bynum, Chris Benson, Al Smith III, Andrew Kubik, Renee Nall and Jonathan Mitchell.

My closest friends are not just my climbing partners. While I have certainly shared a rope with all my dear friends, my adventures with these folks have primarily happened in the horizontal. They have been equally meaningful and these friends have inspired me in infinite ways: Greg Pettys, Amber Hochbein, Bennett and Ashleigh Powell, Amber Jeck, Brittney Jeck, Amy Stevens, Brian Malone, Mike Brenneman, Nate Page, Nathan Kubes and Mike McCarthy.

My yoga teachers have been my spiritual guides, and no doubt have also helped me address and avoid climbing related injuries. Thank you to Brenda Flemming, Lindsey Schauer and Kathy Curran.

Because this is a self published book, I have had to heavily rely on friends to help me edit this. Special thanks to: Lisa Lynch, Jen Panko, Karen Ast, Mary Burt, Mike Reddy, Lindsey Nelson and Al Smith III. Without ya'll, I would have never found my own errors, because in many ways, an artist is blind to his own mistakes.

Much thanks to Lisa Slagle of Wheelie Creative Design, who designed the cover of this book, and Braden Gunem for his craziness and creativity that led to the photo shoot that produced the shot.

And two climbing partners and lovers of life, who left us early, but continue to inspire, in many ways: Josh Burdick and Adam Lawton. I love you and miss you both.

My family has been the greatest blessing in my life. My parents, Lynette and Richard Mehall, have supported me through every challenge and climb, and for that I am eternally grateful. My younger brother, Clint Mehall has been a huge supporter too, and is a mirror into my true self every time I see him. I am also very grateful for my grandmother, Mary Hallman, and my aunts, uncles and cousins.

And to all the girls I've loved before, thanks for the lessons and the love.

ABOUT THE AUTHOR

Luke Mehall searches for his American Dream on the roads and rocks of The West. He is the publisher of The Climbing Zine. His ultimate goal is to inspire people to live close to their dreams. He is a proud graduate of Western State College of Colorado, in Gunnison. Luke lives in Durango, Colorado, where he is a freelance writer, freelance dishwasher, freelance cook, freelance house sitter and aspiring underwear model.

Check out more of the author's writing at:

climbingzine.com

lukemehall.blogspot.com

Made in the USA
Charleston, SC
24 September 2013